THE WAY TO A TRUE

DEMOCRATIC GOVERNMENT

Joseph Alessandrini

THIS BOOK IS DEDICATED TO THE MEMORY OF MY PARENTS GIUSEPPE AND ESTER (NÉE CONTINELLI) ALESSANDRINI WHO SHOWED ME LOVE, STRENGTH AND WISDOM.

TABLE OF CONTENTS

PREFACE

In dealing with the subject of Democracy my approach was dictated by my interest in our existence as sentient beings and the dynamics of our activities and interactions in our approach to life.

CREDO: TO KNOW, ONE MUST LOOK

It is apparent that in life one assumes and advances a *point of view*. Truly, it is ones ability to *see things intellectually* which forms his concepts as a living being. It is how one *views* something intellectually that concludes his understanding.

When one asks another if he understands what was said, the question is, "Do you *see* what I am talking about?" Mental perception and understanding are a shared concept.

What we possess intellectually then, is the ability to *perceive*. One can thereby accurately conclude that knowledge would come from *observation* and would be given to those who would *look*.

Certainty, therefore, would stem and result from: *clarity of observation*.

A *LOOK* AT DEMOCRACY

Any approach to a Democracy must be sufficiently flexible and adaptable to encompass the entire governmental matrix.

In this light, the attempt at a starting point led me to a divide in the road of address; the road to the left said: *"MECHANICS"* and the road to the right was marked: *"CONSIDERATIONS."*

This presented a decision to evaluate and to determine which *look* would provide the preferable route to any useable, workable results in the attempt at the understanding of a Democracy. Workable, only because there exists very little possibility of finding any absolutes when one is dealing with the complex affairs of man.

CONSIDERATIONS AND MECHANICS

In reviewing the subject of "mechanics" we, by necessity, become concerned with the structure and form of how things are arranged or organized; how they are set up to run, essentially how something works, or is working: i.e. the mechanics of governmental systems.

The arrangement of things and how they work would come under the subject of agreements made into laws and the statutes, rules and regulations which societies have made in determining how they will conduct their affairs.

This would have then led to an investigation, analysis and evaluation of the statutes, laws, etc., that were issued by the governing bodies, their history and their current status. It would be a fascinating undertaking for sure, but would it lead us to where we wish to go?

The answer would have to be - no! Why not? The reason is that all the written structure forming our Democratic system of government is a direct result of the ideas, thoughts and considerations conceived by the intellect.

When we look at "considerations" we are in essence dealing with the thoughts and ideas, i.e. the philosophy with regard to the subject matter under review.

Considerations must exist and be accounted for prior to the issuance of any rules for the establishment of a Democratic form of government. This firmly establishes that in the hierarchy of things, considerations must take rank over mechanics as being the senior of the two.

Therefore in dealing with Democratic issues, one must proceed from the *overview* of "considerations," as only by taking an overview are we able to discover its operative principles.

CONCLUSION

The fruitful area then, for delving into and available to provide us with the results we seek, would indeed have to be "considerations."

DIRECTION

In making this determination I have taken the opportunity to avail myself of what I know and to *view* the idea of a Democratic government from the perspective of intellectual address.

"How do we think?" "How do we evaluate what is important?" "What is a citizen?" "What do people want?" "What is the intellectual connection to governing in a Democracy?" These are just some of my many, many questions in the search for possible answers.

PRECONCEPTION

To do this with any bias or slant would have prevented a *clear view* of Democracy as only straight *observation* would guarantee a *clear look* and a discovery of the pertinent facts and data.

In order to achieve a *clear view* I did not think it would be valid intellectually to look for a cause to back or defend, a purpose to support or align with, or a political party to endorse or validate. Indeed, tendentiousness would certainly infer intellectual dishonesty, let the *observations* speak for themselves.

WRITING STYLE

In that I am not much given to prolixity, I tend therefore to lean toward simplicity and hopefully clarity. Accordingly you will find more of a distillation of the areas developed for inclusion rather than an impressive attempt at inspiring erudition. The effort was to isolate the salient points, communicate the findings, impinge, and to be understood.

THE INDIVIDUAL

Although my opinions will and do shine through, I never once abandoned the idea of, and respect for, the value of the individual, his rights and his responsibilities. After all he is "the citizen" and holds the preeminent position in a Democracy.

TO COMMENCE

I begin with a look at the fundamentals of human life, sentience, the intellectual processes, and proceed thereafter to *view* the role of the individual in a Democratic system of government.

Sincerely, J. Alessandrini

"Laws and institutions must go hand in hand with the progress of the human mind. As that becomes more developed, more enlightened, as new discoveries are made, new truths disclosed, and manners and opinions change with the change of circumstances, institutions must advance also, and keep pace with the times. We might as well require a man to wear still the coat which fitted him when a boy, as civilized society to remain ever under the regimen of their barbarous ancestors."

Thomas Jefferson

Introduction

In introducing this disquisition on government and in consideration, and with regard for the foregoing Jefferson quotation I ask for your indulgent forbearance as I feel it is necessary take a brief sojourn into the realm of the intellect, and to thereafter touch upon some of the more relevant facets of existence.

These observations and explanations will enable us to develop and acquire a necessary, broad and deep comprehension; requisite then, to being able to confidently resolve a sound determination for a democratic government.

BOOK 1

Scire Quod Sciendum

The Fundamentals of
Human Existence

Vertebrates, class - Mammalia, order -Primates, family - Hominidae, genus - *Homo*, species - *sapiens*.

Observation and examination reveals the genetic organism to be a biologically engineered, carbon-oxygen engine designed to run on low combustion fuel. The manufacture of energy to enable effort and locomotion are deemed to be its principle functions. It is genetically programmed for survival.

The intellectual awareness of the organism acts as the control center utilizing the body for perception, communication and mobility, thereby making possible interaction: thus the game of life.

"LAWS AND INSTITUTIONS MUST GO HAND IN HAND
WITH THE PROGRESS OF THE HUMAN MIND"

The prescient genius of Jefferson's wisdom comes to pass.

KNOWING

SENTIENCE

Man is a sentient life form. Man in his intellectual capacity possesses "consciousness."

This word comes to us from the Latin word 'conscius' - "knowing, aware" from, *com* - "with" + *scire* "to know."

The base word in Latin is; *Scire* "to know." The original meaning is: *"to divide; to discern; to separate one thing from another; to distinguish."*

To "know" then, in essence, in its most basic, intellectual and conceptual sense is derived from the perceived, singular, defining ability of being able to differentiate, to separate things mentally.

Knowing therefore is a product of the intellectual abilities of *looking* and *distinguishing*.

Thus it can be said that: *The greatest ability of thought is differentiation.*

COROLLARY

Mental clarity is apportioned and achieved to the degree that one can differentiate.

ANALYSIS

The word analysis comes to us from the Greek *"analusis,"* from *"anal-uein"* unloose, from *ana-* 'up' + *luein* 'loosen.'

The dictionary definition of "analysis" is: "A separating or breaking up of any whole into its parts, especially with an examination of those parts to find out their nature, proportion, function, interrelationship, etc...."

ANALYTICAL REASONING, ITS BASIS

In its address to life, the intellect, in order to reason and to evaluate for understanding, must be able to *distinguish* between the differences and the similarities of things in order to compare, evaluate and decide or conclude. In other words, for any analytical reasoning to take place, the *similarities* and *differences* of the subject matter must be recognized and established.

Once done, an evaluation can then take place which is based on relative importance. The evaluation can then lead to an understanding, a conclusion, or a decision for an action.

The intellect has the potential to perform as a perfect analytical mechanism.

NOTA BENE

THE FOLLOWING IS A CONDITIONAL, IMMUTABLE LAW

The ability to analyze for understanding and to discern the correct cause of things is solely dependent upon the intellects ability to differentiate!

THE INTELLECTUAL RECORD: A SIDE NOTE

The registry of the intellectual data available for analysis is entirely derived from the sensory perceptions and intellectual considerations of the awareness of the individual.

Constituting a separate study and not being germane, awareness, as such, will not be entertained. Even, and in so noting, regarding intellectual data input the following will pertain.

AWARENESS: AN ABRIDGED TECHNICAL DESCRIPTION

Awareness is a function of the individual identity; this is the singularity accounting for the differences from being to being and the resulting disparity of data record accumulation: i.e. of what is he aware?

In that the functioning awareness of an individual as a measure of his consciousness is a conditional quality, it differs and varies very widely and very markedly from person to person due to the following:

Our mental attention units could be considered as the life energy quantity of awareness existing within the intellect and as such, they exist in greatly varying quantities from individual to individual. An individual's awareness can range from muted and limited in depth and scope to extroverted, expansive and alert, a scale of very low to very high.

THE SENIOR FACTOR OF INTELLIGENCE

The intelligence of each individual - as befits his uniqueness - differs accordingly. It is obvious and apparent that some individuals qualify as very much more intelligent than the rest of us.

The quality and ability of the intelligence of each individual denotes the monitoring factor for the intellectual process.

Intelligence superintends but does not alter the thinking process.

A simple but accurate definition for intelligence can be noted as follows:

Intelligence: The inherent ability to evaluate relative importance.

VARIANCES

Life experience, education and training constitute individuality and uniqueness but do not alter the basic description of the thought processes so described.

COMMON ATTRIBUTE

The very much earlier above - the description of the intellectual process - concludes the details of analysis and the evaluation of the perceived data.

The above descriptions of the intellect hold true, without exception, for all the life forms of the human race irrespective of race or gender.

ANALYSIS: THE PROBLEM

The faculty of "knowing" is based at origin on the above and it is, and this is important to note: it is a quality and ability not possessed by all members of the human race on an equal basis. People are fundamentally, functionally, and intellectually different.

An inability to differentiate blocks the first step of analysis (analytical or rational thinking) which then leads to a monotone assignment of importance and is therefore productive of, at best, faulty evaluation and conclusion and detrimentally, it will lead to a blocked ability to think or compute in an area.

Thus we get all of the resulting intellectual difficulties and instabilities i.e., an inability to decide; wrong conclusion, mental confusion and dispersion, misidentification, irrationality, aberration, depression, insanity, et cetera.

A BASIC FLAW

To further complicate the matter there is a huge, major underlying *basic flaw of the intellect* - it can include and "compute" or "think" with irrationalities!

IN ADDITION

It must also be well noted that; a computation utilizing incorrect or false facts and information will also yield a wrong conclusion.

These facts or data concealed from the intellectual awareness will cause "identity thinking" so that the power to differentiate and thus to reason is reduced.

Uninfluenced by arbitrary data the intellect is theoretically capable of performing a perfect computation at all times. The data on which it computes may be erroneous, but the intellectual computer is *right!*

INDEED

So noted, the intellect does contain this flaw; that it can "compute" with irrationalities.

How so?

Well, listen to the "brilliance" of Adolph Hitler (a psychopath) then examine his conclusions and actions and then tell me it is not possible!

RATIONAL/IRRATIONAL

Let us draw an imaginary mental line in the intellect and immediately above it we begin to find a bit of reason and rationality, just a little bit, then just below it we begin to demonstrate a bit of irrationality - not too much - just a little bit. For our example then, as we go higher and higher above this imaginary line we begin to find more and more rationality until we ascend to the highest faculties of reason, sanity and survival. As we go lower and lower below this line we find more and more irrationality demonstrating until, at last, we descend into total insanity.

Government is a product of reason and all problems of government can be resolved by reason. Reasoning at its highest level is complete differentiation.

Man has never figured out war, which is insanity. The killing of people goes against and is a reversal of the prime directive of survival. So, war is intellectually, a good example of "below the line thinking" as it is irrational, and yet you will find any number of "reasons why" posited as to "its necessity" by world leaders. This is irrational thinking, this *is* the intellectual flaw!

It has always amazed me to hear politicians and world leaders attempt to justify and to try to apply reason to conducting a war, which is insane as it results in death and destruction, but that is another story.

In an insane world this does not negate the necessity of self-defense and the protection of the citizens of the country from hostile aggression.

TELLURIAN GOVERNMENTS:
A DEMONSTRATIVE ILLUSTRATION

Two aliens out in space were observing our planet. The first alien spoke, "It seems the dominant life-forms on Earth have developed satellite-based weapons."

The second alien asked, "Are they an emerging intelligence?"

"I don't think so." The first responded. "They have the weapons aimed at themselves!"

QUO ITA EST!

—ᴍ—

Extremely Vital Data "Explain" and "Justify"

Fact: It is the basic function of the intellect, at all times, to be *right* and *never* to be wrong!

It is an essential part of human nature to be "right." In the struggle for survival one must always be "right."

When one is confronted intellectually with one's own irrationality and due to being unable to process the information conceptually (this being the intellectual flaw), they will begin to *explain* why it is "right" or attempt to "rationalize" it through the mechanism of *justification*; which is to say, an attempt to make something seem "reasonable" and therefore "right."

Apparently, irrationality and intellectual abnegation are mutually exclusive. When one cannot compute rationally, one would have to admit to being intellectually flawed or wrong! This is something they cannot and will not do *even in the presence of correct data!*

Remember, this is the flaw in the intellect. Compute with irrationality and out will come the dual adjuncts of *explanation* and *justification*. All this is done in an attempt to be "right."

In the kingdom of lies wherein truth be nil
it doth becometh as a poisonous treason.

Says me: "Dost thou thinkest irrationality and truth be somehow conjoined in the realm of the intellect?

Methinks naye, truth be squandered, spurned, defiled, and ne witen in the matrix of unreason!"

* CAVEAT *

It is important, no, it is vital, that I warn you that you must be very, very chary of the originations of the irrational intellect, they are not always genuine; in fact, they will blithely and facilely prevaricate.

Indeed, they feel absolutely no compunction at all about lying and will do so freely!

Intellectually, the higher one is computing with reason the more able one is to be "wrong" and to self-correct to the rational, thus enabling one to think clearly and sensibly. The converse is true when one begins to descend into the irrational levels of the intellect.

So what is the point? When irrational thinking and actions occur, they will result in two things. Please pay very, very close attention here as this is truly vital: you will hear the paired adjuncts of *explanation* and *justification*!

You will hear the most involved and convoluted *explanations* and the most amazing *justifications* which can be just dazzling in their presentation and seemingly impossible to argue with since the amount of emotion usually attendant to their issue is overwhelming.

In sooth, the mendacious politician doth spew forth liberally irrational generalities, festooned and entwined with dulcet explanations and fervent justifications manifest in their complicity.

—⧞—

IDENTITY THOUGHT

"Identify" is defined in the dictionary as: To consider two or more things as being entirely or essentially the same.

The above description of the thought process may stand as written; however, I was aware that it needed to be broadened in scope to be a fully completed concept and to account for much of political and governmental "thinking."

Thus the necessary inclusion of the word "*IDENTIFY*" which will provide for the completed understanding of the intellect and the elements of the thinking process.

It is necessary, and truly, *imperative*, that it be included in pursuing this discussion of politics and a Democratic Government.

EXPLICATION

"Identification" is a substantive, valid factor and must be included in the thought process; where *it is accurate and true*!

So, in the thinking process, we may have differences, similarities, and *where it is correct* the identification of one thing with another i.e. *IDENTIFY*. Thereby, and in thus stating, completing the conceptual understanding of the three principal elements of thought or thinking.

If perhaps seemingly abstract or somewhat abstruse all of the above is nevertheless unquestionably apodictic.

THINKING

The *ability* to think has to do with the *ability* to *differentiate*. An *inability* to think has to do with a *deficiency* in the ability to differentiate and note this very carefully – combined with an *automaticity* to identify things with each other as though they were not only like things, but the same thing!

Identity thought will attempt to identify things which are different as the same or equal; it is irrational!

This last is the area of thinking activity forming the intellectual ambit most favored and occupied by the politician.

All of this with regard to the intellect or thinking is vitally necessary, for what distinguishes man, if it is not that he is a sentient being. Perhaps it would be beneficial to know how he thinks, especially if he is going to govern himself.

IDENTIFY: A GOVERNMENTAL EXAMPLE

One particularly significant reason for the inclusion of *"identify"* is that *this is one of the most basic flaws* in all political and governmental "thinking."

The lowest level of reasoning is a total inability to differentiate; which means to say - identification.

This is the "intellectual reasoning" used in setting forth communism as a method of government.

THE UNDERLYING MISCONCEPTION

This factor of "identify" as a major, underlying reason which prevents political and governmental ratiocination, is to be found deeply imbedded in the subconscious of the race and its origin is to be found in the idea that "we are all one!" This is not true, it is a misconception; it states a false *identification* and in so doing thereby acts to obfuscate and block proper analysis.

Analytical reasoning on a logical basis cannot be accomplished while this idea obtains and the "clear" button for its deletion must be pressed on the intellectual calculator for reason and true justice to come to exist on the individual and thereby political and all governmental levels. For, of what is the government composed, if not of individuals selected from the society?

WHENCE

The source for this misconception is an individual or individuals, lost to history, who then overwhelmed and enforced agreement in all others that this idea was true and existed as fact. This mistaken idea has been carried forward to this day.

It is not true. And, not only is it not sensible, it is an insult! We are individually and definitely, uniquely *different*. You are definitely you and everyone else is not!

Individuals who are firmly implanted intellectually with this idea, and without the ability or the benefit of analytical self-inspection, will tend to think (identify) of government as "the solution."

—⟶⟵—

BOOK II

A POLITICAL SCIENCE?

Political. Dictionary definition: Of, relating to, or concerned with civil administration or government.

Etymology: From Greek *politikos*, of, for, or relating to citizens.

Science. Dictionary definition: A systematically organized body of knowledge on a particular subject.

Etymology: From Latin *scientia*, meaning knowledge.

A literal translation of the definitions and etymologies would be 'A systematically organized body of knowledge relating to civil administration and the citizen.'

What we can deduce from a cursory examination of the definitions above and with putting the words together, we are able then, to see that it has to do with the citizens of a country and a system or arrangement for the conducting of the actions and affairs of these.

NON SEQUITUR

One can mistakenly be disposed to the idea that there is in existence an organized body of knowledge, directed to and useful in the affairs of governing.

Any direct, accurately informed and unbiased observation of the currently existing governmental and political situations — worldwide - will thoroughly disabuse anyone of the idea of the existence of any sort of a - political *science!*

What currently exists politically is called; CHAOS AND CONFUSION; and bears not an inkling or any semblance at all of anything that could even be remotely related to a science!

When operating in confusion, it is necessary to find stable data with which to align things in order to prevent and keep things from being in a chaotic and disordered state. I offer the Constitution of the United States as the foundation document with which to begin.

Additionally, the seminal data offered herein which can be demonstrated as scientific knowledge that can and does help align, and which will prove to be useful and invaluable as stable data: these all acting as beneficial guides by providing the beginnings for bringing about order in establishing a "political science."

SOURCE POINT

The basis for governing and politics has as its origin the Greek, *"polites,"* citizen, an individual of the society.

Politics is based on an understanding of the individual citizen.

A truly simple and uncomplicated concept and yet in practice, its application is foiled by the irrational and aberrant failures of the ideologies and illogical intellectual processes of the politician.

—◆—

Dichotomies

Dichotomies are contradictory things, opposites that offer the opportunity for contrast and comparison and *which form the plus and minus aspect of all thought.*

Some examples are: survive and succumb; beauty and ugliness; right and wrong; love and hate, and politically, *freedom and slavery.*

They offer the opportunity for inspections and assessments from which we may extrapolate to enable understandings.

A CONSIDERED EDUCTION

The following is offered as the plus and minus aspect, the dichotomy, for government.

POWER

Power. Functioning definition: The ability, strength, and capacity to do something.

Question: Where should power be vested, with the individual citizen or with the government?

IF WITH THE INDIVIDUAL CITZEN

Democracy is a form of government. The word comes to us from the Greek word, DEMOKRATIA: Demo, meaning "people" and Kratia, meaning "rule."

The English word is "Democracy." Dictionary definition: (1) A government in which the supreme power is vested in the people and exercised by them directly or indirectly through a system of representation usually involving periodically held free elections. (2) The absence of hereditary or arbitrary class distinctions or privileges.

Thus we have a form of government wherein power is vested in the individuals of the society choosing to be so governed and with no class distinctions.

ERGO

If the answer is to be with the individual then a free, classless society will obtain for the open and fluid movement of the individual based on the ability, initiative, intelligence, and the self-determined actions of each. All such activities are deemed to be motivated and directed in accordance with the prime directive of survival, this being their modi operandi.

Government will exist then to provide the citizenry with the adjunctions considered as being necessary for these survival activities to *freely occur* and *without the added, inapplicable introduction of governmental arbitraries, limitations, restrictions and/or other impediments.*

IF WITH THE GOVERNMENT

If power is to be fully vested with the government then what will exist is essentially a totalitarian state.

Totalitarian. Dictionary definition: Of or relating to a system of government that is centralized and dictatorial and where the state orders the whole life of the individual, requiring complete subservience by the individual to the state.

Nothing else needs to be added to this definition as it stands as a complete concept.

These then are the only two opposite governing possibilities, the first being a democracy and the latter it's opposite.

ITA EST!

All other types of governments which exist, have existed, or can be named, are permutations or other forms of irrational arbitraries of one or the other above.

Under which form of government will "freedom' and "opportunity" exist for an individual?

THE INVERSION

Somehow our politicians have gotten mixed up and inverted the ideas of "govern" and "public servant."

These politicians have the grossly mistaken idea that "governing" means controlling or exercising power or authority over the life of the individual "for the good of all concerned." Please recognize "for the good of all concerned" as two things; a generality and a justifier.

These politicians actually believe that they need to govern as in "rule" or "direct" and "control" and feel they need to take an active role as a ruling agent over the life of the citizen.

This is an inversion as they have not realized they are in public office to serve, to aid and assist the citizens; they are *public servants.*

They are elected by the citizens to serve and assist them in their survival activities; that's what the individual citizens are doing isn't it, attempting to survive?

—⟋⟍—

JEFFERSONIAN DEMOCRACY

In brief, it states the idea and the belief of the goodness of men and the good sense of men in council. It suggests and assumes the belief that men should be free to decide things for themselves. It outlaws tyranny as undesirable and regulates government to the service of the group rather than the group to the service of the government.

PLAUDIT

This is a concise distillation and it is a straightforward yet reasoned view of the role government. It is a model of simplicity to be comprehended, appreciated and to serve as an enlightened concept for those who would serve in the governing of our country.

COMMENT

Only an individual who considers in the higher bands of reasoning will be able to duplicate and to grasp the meaning of these concepts in a direct application to governing.

The full comprehension and understanding of the above concepts - so concisely stated - is unfortunately not available to those who are to be found in the limited, dysfunctional end of reasoning; and they will not be able to come to understanding unless they are shown the way by an enlightened leadership.

Who will lead?

Freedom

The main trouble with understanding "freedom" is that it does not have an anatomy. Something that is "free" is simply "free." It is not "free' with something or "free" from something, it is just and only "free." There can be no qualifiers appending to "freedom."

POLITICAL FREEDOM

Choice. Dictionary definition: A decision to choose one thing, person, or a course of action in preference to others. 2. Power to choose, the ability to choose between different things. 3. A selection or variety of things, people or possibilities from which to choose. 4. An option, alternative, preference or selection.

Definition of 'Freedom' as it pertains on the intellectual level: The absence of necessity, coercion, or constraint in choice or action: Independence.

Freedom is apparently something considered to be highly desirable by the citizens of every nation.

INDIVIDUAL FREEDOM CHARACTERIZED

"This, then, is the appropriate region of human liberty. It comprises, first, the inward domain of consciousness; demanding liberty of conscience, in the most comprehensive sense; liberty of thought and feeling; absolute freedom of opinion and sentiment on all subjects, practical or speculative, scientific, moral, or theological.' Additionally "the

principle requires liberty of tastes and pursuits; of framing the plan of our life to suit our own character; of doing as we like, subject to such consequences as may follow: without impediment from our fellow-creatures, so long as what we do does not harm them, even though they should think our conduct foolish, perverse, or wrong."
-John Stuart Mill

As a nation if we are to restore to the individual his abilities then we must restore freedom. If we cannot restore freedom for the citizen then we cannot restore his ability.

THE POLITICAL VIOLATIONS

Politicians, legislators and government officials violate the "freedom" of the citizen every time they enact and impose legislation upon the society which enforces programs which take away their power of choice thereby not allowing them to decide, choose or opt out on their own initiative. Social, health and economic programs qualifying under "law" comprise these.

You would argue chaos and anarchy and I would contest with "freedom" and the right of the individual citizen to choose. "Legal enforcement" encroaching on the individuals' power of choice is a denial of a citizen's personal freedom.

In dealing with the political organism, the dichotomy becomes: freedom being the plus condition and slavery existing as the minus.

BUT, BUT...

Political statement: "But, there must be conformity for the greater good of all." "We are not all one." I retort, "We are individuals whom God has granted the intellectual freedoms of opinion and choice."

If we are to continue to remain a "free country" the right of the citizen to make his own choices in the determination of his existence must be recognized, granted and fully restored.

The First Precept of a

Democratic Government

The first rule of any democracy and of a free society, and one which must be understood and adhered to by all government servants is:

The individual is ultimately, totally and solely responsible for the condition of existence in which he finds himself, whether it is found to be good or to be bad!!!

In a democracy he will be allowed to *freely* improve that condition. As a citizen in a democracy you have the "right" to be responsible for the condition of your existence in life and your "entitlement" is to have the freedom to change it should you so choose.

UNDERSTANDING THE FIRST PRECEPT
OF A DEMOCRATIC GOVERNMENT

This is the first rule which must be understood and adhered to when governing in a democracy. It must be comprehended and instilled into the governing consciousness of all public officials as it regards the individual citizen. Why? Because only he/she must be allowed to change his/her circumstances if they are not what he/she would like them to be. This is freedom, a freedom of choice. In "your" view they may not be as you think they should be, but it is only his view that counts. The decisions of the individual encompass his responsibility.

The common denominator for any and all individuals is: self-determinism and not determinism by another.

In a democracy the individual citizen must be granted the ownership of and be allowed the freedom to experience his own existence!

This statement does not preclude help. Help is rightly the province of the individuals in a society and not the government. Sympathy can sometimes be a self-serving emotion especially for a "politician," as a way to be elected/re-elected. "What I'm going to do *for* you." Cura te ipsum.

INDIVIDUAL RESPONSIBILITY

The basic, fundamental responsibility for any citizen in a democratic society is minimally: *to feed himself, clothe himself and to provide for his own shelter.*

Let me repeat: The basic responsibility of an individual to himself is: to feed himself, clothe himself and seek his own shelter. It is no-one else's job; it is especially not a job for the government. It is the responsibility of the individual to himself and his symbiotes.

These are the rules of the game of life.

It is not my job to take care of your body, it's yours! This is called personal responsibility.

The first set of conditions which made the United States of America a strong and affluent nation was the individual's responsibility to himself and his family. The government must not interfere in these basic actions which the individual must face in his attempts at survival.

When this precept is violated, the society begins to devolve into governmental interference and control and the vitality engendered by individual responsibility lessens and the society weakens.

"The first requisite of a good citizen in this republic of ours is that he shall be able and willing to pull his own weight." **Theodore Roosevelt**

THE END RESULT OF THE FAILURE OF INDIVIDUAL RESPONSIBILITY

Countries do not bleed, they do not breathe; they can and do behave, oddly enough, like a single organism. But when the individuals in a country cease to behave as individuals, cease to have their own thoughts, cease to be capable of their own initiative, cease to be able to take their own action, then the whole country devolves down to just and only the government; and then it is only the government that can make a decision, it becomes the only thing that can act!

—ɯ—

The Individual, The Citizen

What is an individual? What is he about? What does he want? What does he need? What is he trying to do? We are discussing YOU!

One may state that the intellectual basis for the aforementioned descriptions of the thought processes can and do serve to aid us in establishing the design and purpose of our thinking and reasoning.

The ongoing, continual analysis, evaluation and refinement of the factors of ones existence serve only to forward our survival.

These intellectual doings act to increase, augment and improve our survival activities and the ensuing rewards of proper, valid reasoning are success in our endeavors, enhanced survival factors and an increase in our happiness.

Do not ever give up your rights as a self-determined individual to make your own decisions, make your own choices and do not allow them to be abrogated by any government. This is freedom in a truly democratic society.

There are no guarantees in life, however when you relinquish your responsibility for your survival to the government, you will lose that freedom.

KEY FACTOR: SELF-DETERMINISM

The underlying common denominator for each of us - the very nature
of and possessed by - every individual is: self-determinism.

An individual man or woman possesses two very distinct and inherent traits: the capacity for *self-determinism*, which then demonstrates in his efforts toward - *survival.*

This impulse of self-determinism, to obtain and achieve survival, is what he is all about; *it is the inherent character and makeup of each and every individual.*

THE INHERENT RIGHT OF THE INDIVIDUAL

The activity of thinking is the primary function necessary
to be performed in deciding to make a choice!

What does he need? He needs *the right* to be left alone to make and be allowed to *make his own decisions*; to have the power of choice in determining the direction of, and achieving his goals, in his life.

I emphasize: *He needs the power of choice in leading his life.*

What any individual is instinctively trying to do is survive to the extent that he can, which is all based on his unique capability for existence.

We are all of us different in our thrust or drive for survival and in our intellectual competence. Some of us are more able than others, stronger in will and higher in intelligence, not better, just more able.

This person, the able man, will routinely be attacked by the elements in society which fear any strong or capable individual and yet society relies on the able individuals for its successes, achievements and advances.

To be able to live his life, he has *the right* to be in control of and to be able to freely determine his destiny through his power of choice i.e., to make his own decisions in the attempt at surviving to the best of his ability. These factors encapsulate what there is to understand about an individual in a democracy and life overall.

It has earlier and more famously been said: "Life, Liberty and the Pursuit of Happiness."

FROM WHERE?

The energy of life comes from within and not from without, or by any government decree. This is the essences of life itself, manifest in self-determinism which is guided by the intellectual awareness. To understand a man you must understand his makeup and how he thinks.

Everyone's drive, motivation or urge for survival is noticeably and remarkably different as befits his uniqueness. This is an individual quality this "dynamic drive" and must be accounted for. Some of us are more "dynamic" than others.

This combination of a self-determined drive coupled with intellectual competence varies. Some are very strongly dynamic and others less so. Some are intellectually brilliant and others less so.

The best combination would be high intelligence coupled with a strong, dynamic thrust, certainly not ubiquitous traits. These are the traits which are found in those who are the leaders in all the categories of society.

The dynamics of existence of the individual, well understood by our founding fathers, are well beyond the ken of today's intellectually exiguous politicians.

—m—

Having, How To Have,
The Anatomy Of

Communism: "Everybody owns everything and nobody has anything!"

Politicians undeniably and unforgivably, actively limit the individual's ability to "have" by providing "welfare" and "entitlements." These in effect are perpetuating and keeping him in a lower standard of living. This once again, amounts to a political and governmental betrayal the individual!!

HOW AND WHY

As individuals there are things we need to have - there are things we want to have. In order to have something one must be able to "reach" for it; a concept very much needing to be comprehended.

Reach, an intellectual description: There are basically only *two actions* to be considered intellectually: one is to *reach for* and the other is to *withdraw from*.

The mind is always busy calculating the estimation of these efforts. It is vital to understand this.

Reach, definition, as it pertains: To posses the quality and ability to stretch out in a specific direction in order to obtain something.

ANATOMY

The anatomy of "having" begins with the individual's quality and ability to "reach." The individual's ability to "reach" equals his ability to "have." This is so elementary!

This rudimentary concept must be comprehended in order to build the necessary understanding!

It is the "idea" the individual has to have. It is this "idea" that he can reach which is all important. *An individual is as well off as he can "reach."*

In a truly free and democratic society there must be no limitation thereby allowing the individual the opportunity to reach for and have all based upon his individual desires, interests and needs.

The senior factor above and monitoring reach is: WANT.

Where Do Things Come From?

The "things" in a society are the result of production! They must be produced; production and activity must happen. It is incumbent on the individual to do, produce and work in order to "have."

In the sequence, "doing" comes before "having." It will happen if he can get the idea he can "reach." In a free society, without limitation, he may do so.

What is it that makes a person feel as though he can't "reach?" If nobody else is telling them that they can't reach, they must be telling themselves this! If he can't "reach" then he won't do! And so he won't be able to "have."

You are going to be told by politicians that they can somehow remedy this via legislation!!

Do not be fooled by delusional politicians who would have you believe they can enact some sort of legislative thaumaturgy. Bread and games will only create "the mob."

THE CREATION OF SERVITUDE
POLITICAL SURREPTION

The way to create the state or condition of "reduced or low having" or "non-having" for the individuals of the society is by the prevention of "reach." Just pass legislation in violation of the first precept of a democratic government and it will bring about the condition of "reduced, low having" or "non-havingness" for the individuals of the society.

This will prevent people from "reaching," it will stop them from doing and lower their ability to, and keep them from - "having!" This will ensure a dependency which will surely suffocate any individual initiative and maintain them in degraded and subservient condition.

As the reach deteriorates and the ability of the reach deteriorates, the quality of the reach will then also deteriorate.

This is legislatively imposed LIMITATION!
You may not remove the obstacles to life without bringing
about serious negative consequences

THE CHALLENGES OF EXISTENCE

What conditions will foster a "reach?" The challenges of life and livingness, the responsibility of the individual to himself and his symbiotes will accomplish this. The first "reach" may be a reach for help. But, in order to not be a ward of the charitable institution or person, the individual must become motivated to "act" and if he has any pride he will do so.

This is, in itself, the very source of the vitality of the nation.

"But, but, but what about the unfortunate, poor, deprived troll who lives under the bridge, what will happen to this poor wretch? We are a civilized society and we must take care of him, it's our duty."

Answer: "He must learn to shift for himself; this he is "entitled" to do. It *is* the answer to life and living"

WHAT IS THE VALUE OF SOMETHING OBTAINED FOR NO EXCHANGE?

It is an inflexible fact of reality that obtaining something for nothing is an unbalanced equation - unsustainable in life as well as being indefensible in mathematics.

Have you ever noticed the extremely poor conditions of housing or any other commodities which have been subsidized or have been given for free by the government?

There is no sense of ownership based on personal effort; consequently there is no "pride of ownership." When one earns something that he wants it has value to him and it means something to him, and he will care for it. If otherwise obtained, it stands as proof of his inadequacy and so it will be treated with contempt and disrespect.

NON MAGNI PENDIS QUIA CONTIGIT

—⁂—

CRIMINAL GOVERNMENT PRACTICE

A criminal is one who seeks to get something for nothing, i.e. nothing offered in exchange, whereas an ethical and responsible individual will provide an exchange for what he receives.

All government programs, which in a misguided attempt to "help," seeking to give to or provide to the individual without his doing anything in exchange, is A GOVERNMENT WHICH IS ESSENTIALLY MAKING CRIMINALS OF ITS CITIZENS!

In so doing, it degrades them!

"You poor thing, life has treated you so badly." "You're just a victim of your environment and bad luck." "I think you can't do it so were going to do it for you. Trust me; I know what's best for you!"

"The government will take care of you." "There - you see what we've done for you." "Isn't the government wonderful?"

In actuality, you are being viewed as a non-entity - an object!!!!

A FACTUAL REALITY

One must possess intellectually the faculty of reason in order to think this through to a valid conclusion!

This is a citizenry that is being made the *effect* of its own existence, helped along by its own misguided government.

Life has its challenges and can definitely be a struggle but the obstacles of life must be overcome by effort, intelligence and the application of self-determinism to ones existence. It is not a job for another or the "government" no matter the propaganda you may hear from unenlightened politicians to "help."

This is not help, but is betrayal. In a strong and prosperous democratic society there will always be plenty of assistance and help available to those in need.

"But, but, what are we going "do for" the indigent trolls who live under the bridge?"

—⟋⟍—

BOOK III

Self-Determinism: The Citizen

The "self" is the intellectual identity operating in control of the body.

Determine, it means to decide something. (Refer to earlier; "Analytical reasoning; its basis")

Self-determinism is a condition of determining the actions of self.

If we take any individual man or woman and boil him or her down to their essence we will find this universal impulse called: *self-determinism.*

DESCRIPTION

Self determinism is the common denominator of all human life. This factor comprises the core of his character and is the foundation of his existence.

RELEVANCE

If this factor of self-determinism is well understood it will yield results in providing a basis or starting point for a democracy since per the definition - the individual is "the citizen."

For our purposes then, we can state that self-determinism is *the right of the individual to control his own destiny.* It is a *right!* And, to make his own way in the world as befits his uniqueness; to simply be in charge of himself in his struggle and attempts at survival.

ARCANE TRIVIA

It is pointless to get into any "philosophic" or "religious" discussions as to the "Nature of Man." It being productive of nothing more than a complex, incomprehensible gobbledygook, a Gordian Knot of pure significance and would demonstrate a general confusion and a lack of understanding of the essential nature of the individual; no matter what all the "great philosophers" had to say.

I must however, humbly and appreciably, concede precedence to Gautama Sakyamuni. (563-483 BC) "All that we are; is the result of what we have thought, it is founded on our thoughts, and it is made up of our thoughts."

Weighty tomes and endless streams of words can and do show an overall lack of understanding and therefore obfuscate the basic simplicities of life and man: for *all things worth knowing can and should be reduced to their basic elements, their simplest components, for any understanding to take place.*

If you were to look very deeply and very carefully you would find that what individuals want is the "freedom" to make their own decisions, to make their own choices - to be in charge of and to lead their own lives.

Self-determinism which is allowed to demonstrate can and will lead to self-reliance.

In the attempt to survive and in relationship with others is where the complexity begins; and this is where we must look at the concept of government.

—๛—

LIFE – CAUSE AND EFFECT

As one does demonstrate his existence as a point of view it is necessary to inspect this as a factor to be included in the examination of the individual. In so doing, there are only two ways intellectually to view life in any area of one's existence, one attempt is as a "cause point of view" (more or less) and the other is as an "effect point of view" (more or less).

In actuality, there is only "cause" as one "causes" to be an effect or it could not be experienced, any other consideration would not yield a resolution.

Ordinary people call the assignment of cause "blame." Beware: When one points the finger in accusation or blame you are electing what you selected as "cause" and therefore, since it is "over there" you will hold no sway in that universe; you are now the "victim" and can never be the "victor." You are now the effect of your own assignment of cause.

Simple as a concept, endless in ramifications and complexity, it is the considered source and purpose for our existence as sentient beings: in life experience, one seeks to be "cause" in all things. All of this can and does fold well within the framework and understanding of self-determinism.

LIFES DIVISIONS

One can compartment life into various categories or echelons. The importance of these varies from individual to individual.

In any selected category one can demonstrate more or less "cause." To where one applies self-determinism "causatively" and successfully, he will succeed and will achieve his purposes and goals in that activity and thereby the benefits attendant to achievement. This is the successful individual, the able and competent individual, the foundation of a flourishing society and nation.

THE POLITICAL FAILING

Individuals exhibit varying degrees of causation, some so little as to appear as failures at life's efforts. These appear as marginalized individuals in a society. This area of social reclamation is rightly the realm of the religious organizations so disposed and other humanitarian and charitable activities of a similar nature.

These individuals are not the responsibility of any governmental agency, anywhere, ever!

Why not? Because the attempt to capacitate a lost soul, to make an individual who is weak and failing, come to causation is outside the purview of government; and it can never and will never be able to be legislated into existence. It can only and must be rightfully left to the realm of the Supreme Being and to those so inclined.

Cause, Effect
and Responsibilty

Little understood as a word, responsible has slowly come to mean "blame." However it is a noble word, it is a word graced with honor and dignity. For the individual it means ownership of ones' actions, acceptance of ones causation.

The word "responsible" confers an element of pride in that one is deemed capable of, and able to take action correctly and causatively. A man who is considered to be "responsible" is looked upon as someone who can be depended upon to do the right thing, he is trustworthy.

FULL RESPONSIBILITY: CAUSE AND EFFECT

Interesting as an element of responsibility is the overlooked idea that one is also responsible for *all the actions and all the effects one receives and experiences in one's life*. If it happened to you then you did it, it's the only way out of the maze.

A determination of "full responsibility" is recognition of being causative for both the actions and situations one has "caused" and also for the actions and situations one "experiences" i.e. full responsibility for both sides of the game. In no other wise can an individual achieve complete control over his life.

This aspect of responsibility is the least understood by man. It is an invaluable concept that is rarely able to be conceived. It is little understood, often and usually disregarded and willfully refuted by dimwitted politicians.

THE STEPS DOWN

At the top end of a scale of responsibility then, one is fully responsible for his condition in life. From there, one descends the responsibility scale and from full cause, he then steps down to being responsible only for his own actions (it is here that one finds his "new best friend," the lawyer!)

And from there, he continues his descent on down to: no responsibility for the cause or the effects for his situation in life. It is here, at this point, he becomes the focus and concern of the "Glorious Politician."

IMPLICATIONS FOR THE INDIVIDUAL

An individual is as bad off as he cannot accept responsibility for his own actions and circumstances.

There is a direct ratio between the health and ability of the individual and his willingness to accept responsibility in his life. Any individual is "other determined," i.e. the effect of his own life and existence, to the degree that he will not accept his own responsibility for being alive.

These people are the target audience for the "Glorious Politician" for these individuals will gladly accept the recognition and "help" for their "plight" in life. They make quite a team, the "Glorious Politician" and the "irresponsible." Birds of a feather!

THE CORRECT TARGET

Government must need concern itself with the responsible productive and active members of society, those able beings who are conscientiously attempting to survive; and not those who have given up, or aren't trying, or won't try to help themselves.

"But, but what about the starving troll who lives under the bridge? Have you no human sympathy?"

—m—

Sympathy

Reason and emotion are dichotomies. Intellectually reason takes rank as the senior of the two.

There are *positive* emotions and *negative* emotions.

Sympathy by definition is: The feeling or expression of pity or sorrow for the pain or distress of another.

Sympathy can be described mechanically thusly: The posing of an emotional state similar to the emotional state of an individual in grief or in apathy.

Sympathy is therefore a *negative* emotion.

Technically, emotion is a connector between thought and effort. The more positive the overall emotion of the individual, the higher the *survival* motion or activity level of the individual will be and conversely; the more negative the chronic emotional condition of the individual is, the less activity and motion toward survival will demonstrate.

THE MAKING OF THE "POLITICAL SAINT"

The poor and the woebegone with their tales of failure and misfortune (justifications and explanations delivered in a voice of supplication and pity, all done in a plea for sympathy) are so much more "worthy" of the attention of the "sympathetic politician" in his bid for sainthood.

The competition among politicians in the attempt to publicly demonstrate the most plangent and grandiose exhibition of sincere, humble and deeply felt ruth must be seen to be believed. It can be awe inspiring, I comment snidely.

LOOK AND ANALYZE

However, it is irrational as it is "identity thought."

As stated above: "Sympathy by definition is the feeling or expression of pity or sorrow for the pain or distress of another."

Sympathy is a *negative* emotion and therefore, intellectually, *it will never yield a positive or a corrective result!*

ANOTHER FACT TO NOTE

Apathy. Definition: Is a lack of interest in anything or the absence of any wish to do anything. A person in apathy appears motionless.

In this universe everything which isn't moving is branded as "innocent" and things that are moving are "guilty" - always!!!

This is one of the rationales of the "Glorious Politician" who will "help" the "innocent" and at the same time inhibit the able, capable and productive individuals who do and can produce and are in motion.

In his misguided attempt to "do something" and show his "care" and "compassion" as a "sincere and sympathetic, noble official," he is truly blind to all this but does see his opportunity to establish his own "legacy" as a "true humanitarian." Is he really and truly on anyone's side? Yes, his own!!

"But, but, what about the poor, helpless troll who lives under the bridge?"
"Oh, so cruel and heartless. Why, the shame of it all!!"

Would that it were to be so, that politicians could pass laws banning ignorance, stupidity, incompetence and failure, thereby bringing about true "social engineering."

This unfortunately is well beyond the ken and the power of the legislative body.

The "sympathy" and "compulsion" of the politician to "help" the individuals among us who are termed, "the needy and less fortunate" has been leading us astray as a nation, into a never ending downward spiral.

When emotion rules the agenda reason leaves the room.

—⚍—

Unrelenting Government Direction is: Control

Government legislation concerning the individual is predetermined toward: *controlling bodies* and *protecting bodies*!

These facts are indicative of an inability to recognize the individual and the fact that he is capable of making his own decisions in determining his life.

The individual is thought of as a "body" with no uniqueness, no personality and is the same, i.e. "identical" to every other body; a soulless, mechanistic identification based on "identity thought."

Look closely and deeply and you will find that controlling bodies is one of the underlying, unspoken intentions regarding all governmental actions concerning the individual.

Carried on to its logical end result, as a form of government, we get communism. As in "we are all equally, identically the same!" This is in direct opposition to the basis for analytical thought and reason which is the ability to *differentiate!*

Politically, the understanding of the nature of the individual citizen has been prescinded from reason.

THE PEOPLE

We do not have an indistinct generality known as "the people." This simplicity is an often and usually overlooked distinction by all politicians who talk about "the people." It is an *identification* of the individual. There are no "the people" there is only a nation of *individuals!* This is not just a point which is overlooked, it is *the point!* Politicians and governments never consider the person as an *individual*; they think and speak only about "the people."

This may seem trivial but look where it has got us today!!

MARK THIS POINT CAREFULLY!

Since the beginning of this universe, the end goal of all governments, from then 'til now, is and always has been: TOTAL POPULATION CONTROL!!!

It was ever thus. Do not be so assumptive as to think it otherwise.

—ⱳ—

The Dangerous Politician

The dangerous politician, the one who will work to deny you your power of choice, is the one who says: "But, what about the poor trolls who live under the bridge?" "We must, must, must pass legislation to deal with this social injustice." This, the glaring tocsin of the dangerous politician – beware the master dissembler!

Truly, the only social injustice possible is the passing of laws
limiting the freedom of choice or action of the individual.

The passing of social legislation demonstrates their ignorance and a blatant failure to understand the nature of the individual and the first precept of governing in a democracy which includes getting out of the "taking care of the individual business!"

Delivered as a point of biting sarcasm, the perfect candidate to be championed for legislative assistance by the dangerous politician is: A physically handicapped, mentally challenged, deaf, dumb, blind, female, lesbian, illegal alien, homeless, dwarf troll!

GOVERNMENT DIRECTION

The individual is the foundation of and for any and all Earth societies. The strength of any edifice is totally dependent upon the strength and stability of its foundation. To enable a strong, stable, affluent, society it must be composed of similarly constituted individuals. Thus: *the individual is and should be the focus for societal health.*

"The worth of a State, in the long run, is the worth of the individuals composing it"
— John Stuart Mill

One of the purposes and one of the successes of the American democracy has been to allow the outflow of individual competence to demonstrate itself.

The two general directions to be chosen by government are one: to direct attention to the individuals occupying the bottom rung of society in a misguided plea by politicians to "sympathy" and a personal, political demonstration of "compassion" or two: to direct attention to the upper echelons of the capable, able, productive and intelligent individuals to assist and empower them in creating a flourishing and prosperous society to the benefit of all.

"But, but, what about the starving troll (who won't work) who lives under the bridge?"

—∭—

A Beginning: All Things Must Have
An Origin

EXISTENCE

The basic underlying, singular defining distinction necessary to the understanding of all life forms; what activity every living thing is engaged in and has as its essential purpose once coming into being is: it is trying, it is attempting, and it is *driven to survive*!!

This is life's prime intent, there isn't another motivating principle other than *survive*!!

This must be identified.

Why do I point this out? Because it is the starting point for understanding the nature of the individual. It is the foundational basis of the individual and if it is not understood by the "politician" then all sorts of governing arbitraries will occur.

The difference between a civilization and a barbarism is that in a barbarism there is an absence of any understanding of life itself.

Joseph Alessandrini

INCUMBENT GUIDING POLITICAL PRINCIPAL

In a Democracy, one must understand the inherent nature of the individual and parallel his purposes in order govern well.

IN CONTEMPLATION OF EXISTENCE

In considering your future, would you like to be in charge of your direction in life or are you willing to give up control of your existence to an outside force called government, or "master;" in so doing, you have now become a slave to the state.

"He who lets the world, or his own portion of it, choose his plan of life for him, has no need of any other faculty than the ape-like one of imitation. He who chooses his plan for himself, employs all his faculties. He must use observation to see, reasoning and judgment to foresee, activity to gather materials for decision, discrimination to decide, and when he has decided, firmness and self-control to hold to his deliberate decision."
-John Stuart Mill

—⟶⟵—

The Nature of Things

The primary manifestation which one can note about time and life is a continual and ongoing change. "And this too shall come to pass."

Human life itself is continually engaged in the process of change by means of replacing itself through producing new offspring and the aged and infirm are replaced by a new, healthy and vigorous generation.

Even on an individual basis the old, warn out and damaged cells of the body are being continually programmed for replacement (apoptosis) by new cells thus keeping life invigorated and ongoing.

The essence of life and survival is change. In life all things must come to an end! This is called death! This is life and the nature of all things.

Without change there can be no progress. This cannot be prevented and legislation in defiance of natural law is not just irrational, it is absurd!

Joseph Alessandrini

THE ARBITRARY

Arbitrary. Dictionary definition: Derived from opinion or preference and not based on the nature of things; something which violates natural law; based on random choice or personal whim, rather than any reason or system; A wrong solution held in place by law.

Ideology. Dictionary definition: A system of ideas and ideals, especially one that forms the basis of economic or political theory and policy.

POLITICAL AXIOM

To the degree that any ideology does not parallel or is in non-alignment or does not agree with the facts and realities of existence is the degree to which the arbitraries it concludes and imposes will distort the social order.

CONSEQUENCE

Empowered by their conceited attitudes and elated by their "know best" ideologies, politicians continue to legislate and impose upon us their "ideological views" of society and "what is good for us" even though it be arbitrary, and in direct violation of, and contravening natural law. This is unmitigated, categorical arrogance.

SOME RECENT EXAMPLES

Politicians seek to deny the natural laws of existence by bailing out inefficient and old, worn-out companies ("too big to fail") thus, not only violating natural law but *preventing* newer and better replacements. This results in an ossification of the vitality of the business process to the extreme detriment of society. (Not to mention the overt misuse of public funds.)

"THE LIVING WAGE"

This is one of my favorite arbitraries and a wonderful example of "governments speak" terminology.

Let's address this analytically and do a simple analysis.

LOGIC

Logic. Dictionary definition: Theory of reasoning with the aim to distinguish good from bad reasoning.

Once again the dictionary definition of "analysis" is:

"A separating or breaking up of any whole into its parts, especially with an examination of those parts to find out their nature, proportion, function, interrelationship, etc...."

So basically, we have businesses, jobs, the politician, the worker and the employer.

Bypass. Definition of: In a chain of command or in life when the individual is *bypassed* he is made to be non-existent. His power of control is usurped, whether it be of authority or decision, and he is rendered null.

Both the employer and the employee are being *bypassed* and evaluated for by the politician.

"But everyone needs a living wage" justifies the politician "it's only fair, we must care about the little guy."

WHAT DOES THIS VIOLATE?

To achieve a logical answer one must have the factual data with which to reason and *all relevant facts must be known:* else you attempt to analyze with incomplete data. When data is missing the answer will be wrong and will be looked upon as unreasonable.

Only the business owner or employer can make a proper estimation of the value of a job. To brushstroke with no insight or practical experience for disparate businesses is folly.

Have the standards, qualifications and any needed determinations as to the employability of every individual person been made? Or are they all just humanoid life forms devoid of any intellectual capacity, self de-terminism or any ability to make a decision with regard to their own survival?

TOO SIMPLE FOR EXPLANATION

Any computation for analysis to be valid must include all the relevant data. Leaving out the employers, economic local conditions and types of industries and failure to include the observable differences in the qualifications of the worker is egregious and conspicuously offensive.

The basis of any unreasonable or unworkable legislation is a conclusion made *illogical* when one: OMITS SOME OR ALL RELEVANT FACTS.

By omitting all the relevant facts, *one alters the importance.* In this case, the result is an arbitrary conclusion in violation of the facts and realities of existence.

THE THINKING

"All workers being workers are the same workers in all business circum-stances everywhere and all have the same value as all other workers in all businesses everywhere because they are all workers and all businesses are businesses and all workers shall have a minimum value of $.../hr as they are all workers and we have determined that this is what all workers need to survive - the *living wage*."

This computation, which is a perfect example of *"identity thought,"* concludes the "living wage" which number is established based on no known algorithm, just politically agreed upon opinion.

Ideologically oriented politicians unencumbered by any thought processes and who "know best," attempt to dictate to and overrule the employer in an attempt to show "care" and "compassion" for the "worker."

THE ANSWER

THE ABILITY TO THINK HAS TO DO WITH THE ABILITY TO DIFFERENTIATE!!!

In a free society wherein *different businesses are different,* only the worker and the employer can establish his value or lack thereof!

POLITICAL INTELLECTUAL HANDICAPS, MORE VIOLATIONS AND THE CAUSE

There exists examples of governmentally imposed arbitraries too numerous to mention. However some additional examples of arbitraries are: low income housing, rent controls, price and wage controls, affordable health care, etc.

What do they violate? In a free society, the commercial survival factors of supply and demand are the usual rules by which exchanges are made *and the true causes of the problems these controls were designed to solve were never isolated and dealt with!*

Why not? Because, as was previously and succinctly stated:

Joseph Alessandrini

"The ability to analyze for understanding and to discern the correct cause of things is solely dependent upon the intellects ability to differentiate." And, in addition, "All the relevant facts and data must be included in the analysis to conclude a logical answer!"

In thus stating it serves to point out the obvious, egregious intellectual failings of the "politician."

The Glorious Politician

Any politician who proposes that government is the "solution" for the welfare of the individual is not just misguided but has actually taken on the color of an enemy to personal freedom and individual rights. He must be recognized as such.

Politician. (Actual) Dictionary definition: A seeker or holder of public office, who is more concerned about winning favor or retaining power than about maintaining principles.

Politician. Current action definition: 1. A being who thinks, no, knows, that he "knows best" and that what is best for you and everyone else is what he thinks; all done without validation, consultation or input, vetted only against his own opinions, not facts. 2. Someone who is trying to look or sound important! Leadership qualifications not required.

Politician. Current descriptive definition: A seemingly noble, compassionate and selfless individual who is really just a self-serving man or woman who is motivated, usually and mostly, by personal aggrandizement. A high minded and high sounding perpetuator of: "These people need help and only a cruel and heartless person wouldn't see this and not want to help." This politician needs to find his real calling in life and find and apply to a religious, charitable or social institution and get out of the "taking care of the individual business." Someone please inform him that there is no "sainthood" for a politician. Government has to do with governing. (See some sane purposes below.)

Politician. Current purpose of: To get elected or re-elected.

SOME SANE PURPOSES

To understand the "idea," the philosophy behind the U. S. constitution; to defend the individuals right of "power of choice," his self-determinism and the decisions over his life; to protect the country to keep you safe; to make it possible to educate your children so they may become contributing members of society and succeed in life; to set the rules of governing, devoid of arbitraries in violation of natural law, so that you will be able to make your way in life; to see that the society is without limitation where everyone is free to flourish and prosper to the benefit of all; to install the safeguards of the society.

VALID Q AND A

One may ask, quite fairly, what is the source of my blatant opprobrium regarding politicians and current government?

My answer is: the slowly but surely imperceptible, whittling away, abrogation and disregard of individual rights and responsibilities!

It is inexorable and unnoticeable but nevertheless ever ongoing. And it is being carried forward by the "Glorious Politician." They are "pulling the wool over your eyes" and you go back to sleep. Be thus warned-wake up!

AND

Our "founding fathers" were of a much higher intellectual order than the mental midgets we find among today's feckless politicians who appear to be able to only view life from the self-absorbing, mind-numbing blackness found inside their heads.

Do not be so reasonable as to try to tell me they are trying and it's a really hard and difficult job because then I will know for sure that you are a fool without equal.

CONCLUDING STATEMENT

There is not one true Tribune in existence today among all politicians; no one who would stand up for and protect the rights of individual choice from legislative onslaught. This stands as a black mark against *every single elected official.* No one brave enough to stem and turn the tide back to individual rights and responsibilities. Not one! Anywhere!

Excuses and justification abound! And so I excoriate *all* politicians.

THE STARTING POINT FOR A PUBLIC SERVANT

Before any attempt at being a public servant is even possible, each and every man or woman must resolve and conclude an in depth, soul-searching, personally enlightening, valid response to the following instruction:

PLEASE FIND OUT AND VERIFY FOR YOURSELF THAT IN ACTUALITY YOU EXIST!

LIFE, AN INDIVIDUAL JOURNEY

KEY WORDS

Choose. Definition: To decide from among a range of options.

Choice. Definition: A decision to choose one thing, person, or a course of action in preference to others. 2. Power to choose, the ability to choose between different things. 3. A selection or variety of things of things, people or possibilities from which to choose. 4. An option, alternative, preference or selection.

Decide. Definition: To make a choice or come to a conclusion about something.

Decision. Definition: Something that somebody chooses or makes up their mind about, after considering it and other possible choices.

THE PURPOSE AND PROCESS OF LIFE

The process of life is one of growth, development and refinement.

Intellectually it is a process of life familiarization involving the avenues of survival. It includes explorations of interest, compilation, assessment and evaluation of the data encountered; all of it driven forward by self-determinism and monitored, directed and fueled by the decisions one makes.

Joseph Alessandrini

Life is an ongoing process of analytical evaluation and decisions. The resulting decisions are the determination of one's life.

LIFE'S EFFORT

The purpose of life for the individual is his effort-and it is an effort-in address to the factors of survival to which he can apply his skills, abilities and unique attributes in the adventure of overcoming the obstacles to the attainment of his interests, desires and goals. In this attempt, he will gain personal successes, or not, in his pursuit of survival and in seeking the pleasures attainable from the joys of livingness.

THE POTENTIALS FOR EXISTENCE

Whether considered by him or not, everyone is engaged in a continuing life-process of learning, understanding and self-discovery as it relates to his existence and his survival in this world.

ARENAS FOR ACTIVITY AND EXPLORATION

In this activity of existence, he has the opportunity and potential to learn about himself in regards to himself; with regard to his family and different groups of people as well as his kinship to mankind and life, the physical universe, the spiritual side of his existence, and perhaps to the greater concept of infinity or that of a Supreme Being.

All of this encompassing an ever widening sphere of personal interest and providing the opportunity for personal expansion.

It is an inviolable right and one must reflect on this as his chosen journey, again, whether this has been consciously considered by him or not.

It is a singular journey undertaken exclusively and resolved solely and only by oneself. It is a self-discovery process of experience for one and all; for in the end you will be the result as you are, alone with yourself for better or worse.

This evaluation can only be made by the individual for himself, for when it comes to himself, only he truly "knows." All that is available and achievable to one, all he will ever get out of his life is himself; and sometimes one may find, at the end of this journey, that he is unsatisfied with his result.

"Excellence is never an accident. It is always the result of high intention, sincere effort, and intelligent execution; it represents the wise choice of many alternatives - choice, not chance, determines your destiny." ARISTOTLE.

POLITICAL INTERVENTION

You have your lifetime to travel this adventurous journey and where and how you end up is up to you and it is predicated upon the *decisions* you make and the *choices* you make in leading your life. It will not be the result of any legislative direction or by the grace of any governmental decree.

This journey will be affirmed exclusively by, and it is particularly and peculiarly defined as: *the summation of the totality of the decisions one makes in his life and no other factors.*

Your *decisions* and your *power of choice* are your most valuable and prized possessions!

In leading your life, you must not allow politicians to lead you astray using glibly captious and otherwise persuasively slick, political sophistry.

You are the cause and result of your own decisions and the choices you make. *This is true freedom in a democracy given survival as the goal and barring governmental interference regarding intrusion into the personal and private actions and activities of your everyday living.*

Once again, you are ultimately responsible for the condition in which you find yourself; thus it always has been and thus it always will be!

DECISIONS

The important, meaningful decisions upon which life evolves intellectually are brought about by the exigencies imposed by existence and survival.

—⟶⟶—

A PHILOSOPHICAL LOOK: LEVELS
OF INTELLECTUAL AWARENESS

For those individuals who are come to achieve the beginnings of self-awareness ("cogito ergo sum") there are existing, higher echelons of understanding and awareness available through intellectual insight; all roads leading to "knowing" in the fullest sense of the word.

Every individual possesses the innate capability for intellectual and ethical perfection: these being the goals of past sages and the principles or guiding philosophies which encompass all religions.

Unfortunately for the politician this road to enlightenment is barred for, by necessity, it must begin with an understanding of life. Thus my instruction to them: "Find out that you EXIST!"

—⟶⟶—

The Establishment of Order

ANY ACTIVITY IS A DIRECT FUNCTION OF ITS PURPOSE.

Purpose. Definition: The reason for which something exists or for which it has been made or done.

GOVERNMENT PURPOSE

If one is able to ascertain the purpose or purposes of something, the activity or thing in question, then the answers will reveal themselves as to the outline, makeup, direction and function of the activity and will go to establish the resulting overall delineation of the activity and efficacy of the office.

A simple question of: "What is the purpose of…? What are the purposes for…?

"What is the purpose of government?" "What are some purposes of government?"

These are questions that will begin the process of discovery. These things can be identified and named.

PURPOSES OF THE POSITION

Every government position, every elected official from the President of the United States on down has a purpose or purposes for the job he is doing. These purposes need to be discovered, delineated and issued publicly so that at least we would have some idea of what they are supposed to be doing and whether or not they are achieving these!

They need to, and they must, align with the overall purposes of government. If they are not found and publicized then we are left with every new person elected to office bringing his own ideas of what the job should be. We are now open to ideological arbitraries, personal opinion and irrationality.

EXAMPLE

From the presidential oath of office: "*... and will to the best of my ability, preserve, protect and defend the Constitution of the United States.*"

This goes to point out one of the major purposes of the office of the President of the United States of America.

GUIDING PRINCIPLE

Agreed upon aligned purposes bring direction and order leaving initiative and creativity on how to achieve them to the official duly elected.

Democracy An Ideal Scene

In a true democracy there would exist a free and therefore fluid society. Each individual will be, and must be, allowed to find his place based on his personal interests and desires, his unique abilities, level of intelligence and self-determined motivation.

As long as it is a fluid society, then there can be no "class" designation; each according to his desires and ability to create, and the freedom to choose his survival direction in a society *without limitation.*

You will find yourself where you place yourself by your own action and you will be free to change as you wish.

This stands in opposition to the designations of: upper class, middle class and lower class, ideas which have been inherited from other cultures and which are perpetuated by divisive and self-serving politicians.

TRUE FREEDOM

In a free and fluid society based on initiative and the demonstration of competence anyone can place himself or move freely up or down in distinction; it is a self directed proposition. Economically, socially and geographically you will be where you choose.

ANARCHY

There are those of you who will read this and assume incorrectly that what I am talking about is anarchy. This is a gross misassumption on your part as nothing could be further from the proposed outline.

Anarchy. Definition: A chaotic situation, a situation in which there is a total lack of organization or control.

Those who fear a free society composed of self-determined individuals will seek to impose restrictive controls in order to "Guarantee safety and security" "Order and control" and so that "No one will be able to take advantage of another" and "Where we will all be equal." and "We will protect and help you and take care of you." "We need a level playing field so it will be "fair" to everyone and no-one will ever have more than anyone else. We must bring equality (Like in communism)." "We must prevent anarchy. We must establish a "correct" and "just" social order."

Sayeth the Glorious Politician: "What would happen if everyone was free to do what they wanted to? We can't have that. We must stop this from ever happening; we must impose order and control."

Ordnung muß sein!!!

HOW WILL IT HAPPEN?

This will always be done via oppression disguised as "Enhanced Social Order" or some such euphemistic expression, but nevertheless it will impose government legislation and limitations without choice and other population control mechanisms "for the good of all."

Remember, the direction, the focus, the end game for all governments is: "COMPLETE AND TOTAL POPULATION CONTROL."

This, unfortunately, can only be achieved through suppression of the individual by limiting his self-determinism. Thus we will have neither a "free society" nor a democratic one. Dispute this at your peril.

AS ALWAYS, IT'S UP TO YOU

Some of the true purposes of a democratic government are to provide protection and set up the rules of the game to enable and ensure that equal opportunity exists for the prosperity and welfare of all of its citizens i.e., no limitations.

Anyone's life and existence is predicated on the basis of what he produces and contributes to life. Your life is like your own personal bank account, you only get to withdraw what you contribute to it. Some do not put in anything or very little and others contribute greatly. Government can only act to skew the equation.

In 'the true democracy' the individual can never be considered to be the responsibility of the state.

A true democratic state exists at the behest of its citizenry and is created to administer to the affairs of the body politic. It does not exist, nor will it ever have as one of its purposes, to be a life support system - that is socialism and not the American Democracy. A democratic government does not have as one of its functions to provide succor to any segment of the populace, this is a private sector activity in alignment with the mission and purposes of charitable, religious and other designated humanitarian organizations.

Once again, it is your life and you are ultimately responsible for the circumstances and conditions of your existence. So be it!

—m—

HELP

Help. Dictionary definition: To make it easier or possible for somebody to do something; to provide assistance.

All of us, at one time or another, have been the beneficiary of help in some way and also we have done so ourselves in assisting others. It is a common social impulse.

A POINT TO CONSIDER

When help extends beyond the point of helping the person past the time of need, it becomes something else. It becomes a tether to the helper thus restricting any need by the individual to improve or change his condition.

Ongoing, continual help will perpetuate the liability of the situation. This is why government welfare programs are a limiting factor in our society; they truly do not "help" but go to perpetuate a non-optimum situation.

"Help" from the government that amounts to a handout, is really no help at all. It only serves to make the politicians' feel good about themselves and to, in some perverse way, make up for their self-serving interests.

THE ONLY TRUE HELP

The only true and lasting help is: *self-help*! It must be intrinsic, and thereby, it can and will become ongoing and permanent; it can be encouraged and nurtured but first and foremost: *it must be fully recognized as not being adventitious!*

HELP FROM WHERE?

It is only in a flourishing and prosperous nation will there be help and care for those in true need.

The people of the U.S. are the most generous and helpful of any nation in the world. Charities and other non-profit organizations that have as a purpose to care for those of us deemed "the disadvantaged" and in true need, have always been assisted by those of us who can and are able to care. It is a common social impulse. *This help can only be guaranteed by a truly prosperous nation.*

WE ARE *DIFFERENT*

Individuals are different, they possess different capabilities. We may be born with equal rights under the law but we are not all born equal or the same, this is "identity thought;" some are more able than others.

And, if you think all individuals in a society are "trying," then you are mistaken and have become "reasonable" and are fundamentally deluded.

Sympathy is a poor excuse for understanding the nature of the individual

A SIDE NOTE ON HELP

One could reasonably assume that everyone is dedicated to their own survival. Seemingly not understandable but, this is patently not true! This is a manifest error made by one and all. Not everyone is trying to survive!

The Way to a True Democratic Government

Trying to help someone to survive who is really trying to succumb is truly vexing but nevertheless, problematic to both the helper and the person being "helped!"

Yes, it is truly very baffling and certainly not sane but it is a fact of life which must be accounted for in any society as many of these individuals are extant; more than one would reasonably presume to be the actual fact.

—⁓—

The Thoughts of a Parent

In the having and in the raising of children, any concerned and responsible parent wishes to see their children grow up and blossom into responsible, self-reliant and successful adults.

Their desire is that they become individuals who are capable of making their own decisions and leading their own lives and no longer needing their hands to be held as they once did as children.

Why do politicians refute this concept and conceive that citizens need their hands held through adulthood?

Politicians, as befits their intellectual handicaps, have a limited and short sighted view of the nature of an individual and insist on making decisions for them; undeniably, it does serve to advance their self-serving, vote getting intent.

Indeed, as they are so blinded by the glare reflecting from their self-projected brilliance, politicians' possess, at best, an oblique view of life and no insight at all into the very nature of the individual and what constitutes the makeup of a free society.

Short changed intellectually, politicians are intent on imposing their personally conceived and arbitrary ideological opinions on how a society should function, and in doing so, the individual as well as the society are both suffering.

CHILDREN

Self-important, cunning politicians knowing full well that *"children in peril"* stories are pure gold, will look to bask in the glory of these *"sympathy exciters,"* using the opportunity to grab headlines and to seek public acclaim. As it is premeditated and is being done intentionally, it is simply an unabashed, devious attempt to garner votes or to advance their phony public façade as a 'sincere and truly concerned, humble, caring citizen!' – And, "Remember to vote for me in the next election."

The political projections of: "What about the children?" "We've got to protect the children." "What about the starving children?" "We've got to save the children" and countless other banal, unimaginative declamations are continually being voiced by hypocritical, publicity seeking, do-gooder politicos.

TRULY

Children are and have always been the responsibility of, and belong in the care and control of their parents. In a democracy they are neither under the dominion of, nor the responsibility of the state.

"Again, you heartless reactionary, you would let the trolls children do without and go hungry and starve. How can you live with yourself?"

I politely refer you to the "The first precept of a Democratic government."

TE VOLUNTATE

As a politician, if you feel a personal, individual need to perform some generous, charitable act based on your own volition and from a personal sense of responsibility, then I will applaud your effort.

However, please do not place a burden on society based on your personal idealism.

CONTRARY FACT

Were these dysgenic politicians to be truly honest about their care and concern for our children and the future generations they would cease to relentlessly burden them with a massive and unsustainable debt structure. This they could actually do something about; but no....

They avoid this fact and when confronted about it they blithely ignore the issue, shamefully "justify" their ways and continue on with their irresponsible spending.

Short sighted thinking is too polite a description.

CHILDREN, POLITICOS AND THE "ROLE MODEL"

The label "role model" is posed by politicos and projected upon a famous person or a famous athlete and is then referenced to children. As though children have no sense and will do and act *exactly* like the famous person in all respects equals "identity thought," the mainstay of political thinking.

Setting a good example is definitely a positive for any individual but of greatest importance is the immediate environment of the child, i.e. his family, as this is where his identity and social habits are formed.

It can only be termed "political grandstanding" by those politicians who seek to ride the coattails of the famous and admired individuals and yet, who can't seem to perform to their own ideals.

It appears to be that they only lie when their lips move! (Unfortunately, the real problem with political jokes is that they get elected!)

—m—

BOOK IV

EVIL

Evil, does it really exist and if so, what is it?

Yes, it does exist and... What is it?

It is the intellectual dramatization of *evil purposes* or of *evil intentions*!

It is a purpose or an intention contained within the intellect that seeks to educe the means to harm or destroy.

There are in existence and walking among us in all earth societies, *evilly intended beings.*

THE EVIL ONE

Evidence of these purposes and intentions can be found in anyone but:

There are in existence among us beings, whose every thought process is wholly engulfed by, and whose every conscious moment is consumed and driven by, their evil intent.

For such beings, their evil intention to harm or destroy is the overriding and continuous motivation of their existence. It never shuts off, it is always engaged, it never abates; it is their single-minded, full-on mindset!

WHY

In their own delusional minds they think they are *continually* surrounded by others who are trying to "do them in." They live in unsuspected terror, *everyone* is against them. They are *covertly* insane! They exist in fear and terror of *everyone* and they mean to harm or destroy you. *It is not ever otherwise!*

They are in a perpetual contest with everyone as they conceive all are enemies out to destroy them. They exist in an inconceivable, delusional horror exceeding the boundaries of belief!

This constancy of their evil impulse is the controlling and driving factor of their existence.

FALSE IMPRESSION

What image does an evilly intended being conjure up in the average person's mind, an image of a person with horns - fangs - and long, sharp bloody fingernails, a Great Earl of Hell? This is completely, patently, and absolutely - not so!

They are beings who are *covertly hostile* and will seldom act to be discovered by being openly violent. They *live in terror* and they *fear everyone*!

They fear us all and especially anyone who is powerful and who can thus possibly act to destroy him or her. They are unsuspectedly, continually, and secretly at war with everyone — always!

They gravitate to sources of power and influence and will seek to bring them down.

They walk among us and cover their intent with a veneer of social acceptability. This allows them to exist in full view, act and participate in all walks of life and still act on their covert intent to harm or destroy.

"I am the Spirit that denies! And rightly too; for all that doth begin should rightly
to destruction run;
'Twere better then that nothing were begun.
Thus everything that you call Sin, - Destruction in a word, as Evil represent - That
is my own, real element."
— J.W. von Goethe

INTELLIGENCE

Intelligence is not a clue for the indication of an evil being; they can be bright or stupid or average. If they are extremely intelligent they can rise to considerable heights in any field, they may even become head-of-state.

"If only one man dies of hunger that is a tragedy. If millions die, that's only statistics."

"Death solves all problems-no man, no problem."

— Ioseb Besarionis dze Jugashvili, Joe Stalin, "Koba,"

Do not be fooled, the bulk of these evilly intended beings exhibit no outward signs of insanity. They can and appear to be quite rational. They can be *very* convincing.

HARSH REALITY

To the rational, reasonable mind the above description of an evil being does not seem possible, it truly does not compute and really, it just doesn't make sense! Of course it doesn't, it's not just irrational; it is the severest and most extreme form of insanity!!

Do not attempt to make sense out of it, you can't; it is full-on evil, get it?

—⚏—

Joseph Alessandrini

Their evil intent and motivation places them beyond the bounds of compassion or sympathy. Would you be nice to the Devil? Well the "Devil" exists and he has taken on human form in the guise of the evilly intended being. One cannot reason with evil insanity, there can be no justification found for it- ever!

Label them and expel or convict. Never, ever sympathize or try to "understand" as there can be no "logical explanation" or justification – ever!

Do not attempt to apply reason to abject insanity else you will be demonstrating tacit agreement and now you yourself are become suspect.

A VERY SMALL PERCENTAGE

Whereas greater than 80% of us are normal, well intended individuals and attempting to survive in harmony with our fellow man, it is unfortunate for us there are individuals in the world who are "bad guys!" They are the ones who are responsible for evil and the cause of chaos in the world

They live in unsuspected terror and are driven by their evil intentions; and please note this well - they fear *everyone*. To such a being, every other being is an enemy to be covertly or overtly destroyed. *This is especially true of those individuals who are powerful, strong and able, since these will cause him to suffer the utmost agony of personal danger.*

These evilly intended beings are small in number, amounting to only about 2-3 % of any population.

They can, and do, influence others and cause them to become swayed and engulfed by the evil they intend. These thralls then, account for the remaining percentages.

HOW?

This evil is done covertly, secretly, and especially not openly, to enable escaping being discovered.

If you think wars and genocide come about "naturally" then you have become reasonable regarding the fact that some people are truly and viciously, evilly intended. They mean you harm and if you are powerful they mean to destroy you. A "turn the other cheek" attitude is not the way to deal with these types.

One must "face up" to this fact and recognize it for what it is. There is evil in the world and it comes from somewhere, do NOT think otherwise! It comes from some of your evilly intended fellow men. They exist and they influence those around them susceptible to their influence.

The evilly intended cannot create, therefore they cannot generate any power on their own and so, they will gravitate to the sources of these. They exist amongst us in every strata of society and it is vital to note that the targets for these evilly intended beings are: the power lines of government/politics and economics/money. Is it any wonder that these two areas are the most involuted and confusing, both apparently lacking in knowable certainties and causing the most in the way of disruption for our society and the individuals in it?

Economic turmoil, domestic strife, and wars are the products of these beings. These things do not "just happen" they are *caused!* It is truly, vitally important to understand this; it is not "Satan" or "God's will" but the viciousness of evilly intended men. They do exist. One must be very, very watchful.

SOME CHARACTERISTICS

They will speak in very broad generalities: i.e. "Everybody thinks..." "Everyone knows..." "They say..." This will be natural to them since all of society is a hostile generality against him/her. The people around this person will not be doing very well, they will be ill, or behaving in a crippled, submissive manner in life.

Interestingly enough, an evil being cannot finish an activity once begun; they cannot bring things to completion, this is a quite odd indication.

"The smiler with the knife beneath his cloak."

— Geofrey Chaucer

This is the evilly intended individual who says with a sincerely - insincere smile "I just want to be your friend." Watch for the knife behind your back. They are *covertly* hostile.

EVIL: COMES THE REVOLUTION

The evilly intended revolutionary is a subversive who will promise a people freedom and equality and instead gives them eradication of their best minds and cultural institutions; to the end of a totalitarian regime.

WHO FOLLOWS?

The subversive leader can only use people as his recruits those who are influenced by and aligned with his intentions; if they did not exist he would have no personnel. To such people the perfidious and twisted practices of subversion have an enormous appeal.

By destroying the church and other institutions or by holding these up as nothing, it sets these types above any necessity to conform to an existing social order. Thus the thrall is exhilarated by a new justification for doing on a wider scale what he normally does; nullifying by hidden and insidious means all the strong and orderly found in the environment.

In any barely civilized social order or one of limited sophistication, the idea of having the right to do hidden and vicious things in the name of the "Glorious Cause" is so attractive to these types that they are drawn to and will automatically support this political idiocy

THE PURGE

As reason is absent from these individuals it never occurs to them that the most zealous among them will be the first to be "eliminated" since even a totalitarian regime must compel severe conformity to it's own "codes" no matter how depraved they may be. The selection will be made by his continuing revolutionary desire not to conform to any set or regimented patterns.

WHY?

The morbid fear of any totalitarian regime is - counter-revolution!

COMMUNISM AND EVIL

The evilly intended personality has a very bad sense of ownership and property. They conceive that the idea that anyone "owning anything" is just a pretense made up to fool people. They know that nothing is really ever owned. "Everybody owns everything." is just another generality!

These evil beings are *covertly* hostile, not generally openly angry. Their evil intent can be hidden behind high minded rhetoric and other idealistic sounding phraseology. This individual is quite certain, and presents in his warped and perverted view, that he is "acting for the best" and commonly presents himself as the only "good person" around, doing all for "the good of everyone."

From Karl Marx to Lenin, Stalin, Mao Zedong, Kim ll-sung, Castro, et alia, they all have been and are the evilly intended, revolutionary leaders of every communist takeover on the planet as this means of "government" ensures that no powerful individuals will emerge.

They have a strong, deep fixation that their survival depends on keeping others down or keeping them ignorant. They are covertly, viciously evil, they fear and seek to suppress all.

Communism as a social culture is the welfare state at its worst. The creation of indigence in the population makes it easier to control. It exists by the nullification of strong individuals in the society, the removal of all constructive persons and the preservation of the idle, the hopeless, the helpless and the weak.

Communism and the idea of individual liberty exist as an oxymoron, perhaps now you can see and understand the underlying fundamental as to why.

THE PRICE OF INDIVIDUAL FREEDOM
IS A CONSTANT VIGILANCE

Do not be deluded, please do not follow or accept the idea that *"everyone is good"* as unfortunately, everyone is not "good!"

You are now duly informed and have been alerted to *the prime source of all of our societal and governmental ills.* Look very deeply and very carefully, do not be reasonable - ever. Evil does exist and it does have a source - it is the evilly intended being; you have now been forewarned and fully apprised.

—⚏—

Abundance

THE SOLE GUARANTEE FOR SURVIVAL IS ABUNDANCE FOR BOTH THE INDIVIDUAL AND THE NATION

The expression "the rich" has been made into a pejorative term by those politicians who would hoodwink the general populace into thinking that those persons who have placed themselves in a position where they can provide for themselves and their family in a secure fashion, the innuendo being they have done so by devious, nefarious means.

Everyone would enjoy being "rich." A good example to review is the current popularity of the state lotteries, which really amount to a tax on the poor. Why would the "poor people" play a lottery?

So they will be "rich!!" It is a simple, universal impulse to not be "in need." Who would not enjoy the benefits obtainable from financial freedom?

AIR, FOOD AND WATER: LIFE'S ESSENTIALS

Do the "rich" breathe more air than anyone else? Do they eat more food and drink more water than anyone else so as to cause deprivation? Do the roads they drive on wear more due to use by the "rich"? Do they have an undue strain on the public services provided in their communities? Do they personally utilize more of our natural resources because they are economically viable?

Joseph Alessandrini

The answer is no, not any more than any other individual in society.

So why are they singled out by politicians to provide a disproportionate amount of their income?

Why should success in the economic arena subject an individual to a penalty of a disproportionate tax burden?

Would that it were to be so that politicians were just as interested in asset creation as they are in the asset distribution called "tax the rich."

WHY?

The glib, politically correct answer (read 'justification') is "because they have "so much" or "too much" money and "they can afford it" after all they are the "rich" and so they need to pay their "fair share" and one of my favorites, "They need to give back," that all seems very reasonable doesn't it?

In consecution the correct and accurate answer is because they are *successful* and are therefore *targeted!* There really and truly is no other verifiable or supportable reason beyond that.

—m—

Fair. Definition: Reasonable, impartial or unbiased.

Unbiased. Definition: Free from partiality or prejudice; fair.

Impartial. Definition: Not favoring one more than another; unbiased.

"Oh, you've got it so we'll take it."

Most successful people started or set up long enough, and worked hard enough, to become sufficiently successful and in so doing ensuring an abundance for themselves and their families.

They generally contribute more to their chosen fields and so are rewarded monetarily.

What is unfair is they are now supposed to make up for those who do not; certainly this is unfair.

It is an unbalanced equation in any mind exhibiting a modicum of common sense; except for those intellectually dysfunctional politicians who supposedly seek the admirable but unachievable idealistic goal of "social justice and economic equality."

THE ACTUAL REASON

In an oppressive society the able will always be a target for the evilly intended. In the world of international relations the wealthy countries, such as the U. S., will always be the target of the 'have not' nations led by oppressive leaders. "Attack the able" is their mantra. It is motivated solely and only by their "evil intentions." Do not be so foolish to think it is otherwise, regardless of the rhetoric involved.

"THE RICH"

There is no real world definition for "the rich" it is just a snide generality utilized by the evilly intended politician (remember him?) who would covertly attack and bring down the successful individuals of our society.

A PROPER DETERMINATION

Any forthright, conscientious look into the field of successful men will show that nearly all success is more than adequately deserved.

HOMEWORK AND SOME RESEARCHED DATA

The long time director of an imposing institute of psychology revealed confidentially, that when he first entered his profession that to some degree he was convinced that the capitalist, the big industrial manager, and the director of the great corporation, had all arrived where they were because of luck, avarice and carelessness for the feelings of others.

Auspiciously the facts of reality proved otherwise, as the following will illustrate.

FINDINGS

During the course of the ensuing years he personally or through his staff had done extensive industrial psychometric testing of many organizations. By means of this work he had an opportunity to test a great many of the capitalists, managers and industrial giants of America measuring their mental traits, capacities and processes.

As a result of the testing what he discovered was that the endowment of these individuals included: *a rich appreciation of life, a great feeling for their fellow men, and an enormous persistence coupled with intelligence in planning and execution.*

What had become apparent to him: "Those who were at the top very well deserved to be there."

His conclusion was that the world was carried on the backs of a few desperate but very big men; and that luck was not chance.

TAKE AWAY MESSAGE

We are not all the same nor equally endowed - some of us are more able than others.

—ຶ—

Production and Taxation

Taxation has become an open ended liability passed on to the citizenry by fiscally irresponsible politicians. Once again the able, capable and productive members of our society will be burdened with a "your fair share" guilt trip take away: a euphemism for governmental confiscation.

When you penalize production you will get less production! This is an unalterable fact!

You have been "programmed" into thinking that taxation is in someway right, just and somehow necessary. While it is true that we all must share in the responsibilities we assume for our defense, public works etc., it stands that the process of taxation has been abused by purblind politicians to a burdensome, detrimental effect on the welfare of the individual and thus the nation.

It has passed on the abuse of profligate spending to the citizenry because it cannot exist within its budgetary controls as must any individual, business or corporation. And so by subreption, politicians instilled this idea in your consciousness in order to take away your money to fund the government's excesses at the expense of the individual's ability to fund his own family's welfare!

FAIR AND EQUITABLE

Limitation. Definition: A restriction, the action of limiting something.

Our current United States progressive income tax policy is a cleverly de-signed "limitation" on the earnings of the able individual. It is essentially a means of income redistribution-period!

"Fair and equitable" is just a way to make those who produce - pay more! It's a take away, communistic proposition designed to burden and bring down the able individual. It is a penalty for being competent and suc-cessful and it must be recognized as such.

"Fairness" politically, just means we are all beholding to the government to becoming all "equal" and "one."

We are not all "the same."

—∾—

The "Glorious Politician"
The Self Proclaimed
"Champion of Social Justice"

"I'm just a really good person who cares about the little guy." So announces the self-important and condescendingly arrogant Glorious Politician.

Equal. Dictionary definition: Being the same in quantity, sized degree or value

Fair. Dictionary definition: Reasonable or free from bias.

If in the eyes of the "Glorious Politician" we were "all created equal" and we are all "entitled to the same things as everyone else" and yet they all fail to notice or deliberately overlook the fact that the "created equal" non-producers are not contributing their "fair share" to the public trough. What then is the justification for allowing them to be given what they have not produced and are not entitled to?

Why is it that the bottom rung of society is not holding up their end if they are "equal?"

The "Glorious Politician" can't have both ways; if "everyone is created equal" then the non-producers need to get off their collective "duffs" and pick up the slack and contribute to society in some meaningful and productive way.

Individual life itself, left as the final arbiter, will correct this situation if politicians will only adhere to The First Precept of a Democratic Government. "Need" has been and always will be the ultimate motivator as it is backed by the genetic urge to survive. Everyone must seek his own way in this world.

Glorious Politician: "Oh no, but what about the poor, downtrodden troll, what is he to do?"

Reply: "He must work and earn his way."

Glorious Politician: "Oh no, that's just not fair."

Reply: "Who is the man who said that life is fair?"

FAIR

Those successful individuals in our society already pay more in taxes-how so?

By earning more they pay, even at the same rate, a higher amount in actual dollars.

So the idea that the so called "rich" should have to pay even more in taxes is really an idea put forth by evilly intended politicians and has no basis in "fairness" or "equality" but recognize it for what it is; an oppressive levy enforced on the able, productive members of society, it is a *limitation* and it is imposed only on the able, productive, succesful individual.

INTELLECTUAL ILLUMINATION

"...a wise and frugal government..., shall leave them otherwise free to regulate their own pursuits of industry and improvement, and shall not take from the mouth of labor the bread it has earned." Thomas Jefferson.

We have not a "wise and frugal government" and it is taking away "the bread it has earned" from the individual.

The Level Playing Field,
Fairness and Equality

The game of politics as it is currently administered.

Any society as a whole will always be segmented as any rational individual would expect.

This will usually be viewed from the evaluation of socio-economic conditions. It will have a top stratum, a middle division and a bottom rung. This *is* how individuals will naturally settle out and arrange themselves when left to their own devices in a society without class distinction, and without interference from the government.

This is the natural order of things in a free society since every individual is unique, has different capabilities, needs and desires - we are all *different*.

Political ideologues however, having their unusual and strange ideas, seek to impose their "ideologies" and to foist via legislation irrational "arbitraries" on all of us in an utterly impractical attempt to make everyone "equal," this once again can be seen as a violation of the natural order of things.

SOCIAL ENGINEERING

There is an ongoing attempt by politicians to bring down the top echelon of successful, competent, productive individuals through the imposition of burdensome taxation: "Everybody should be, and must be, taxed-according to his ability to pay." And, to "lift" the bottom rung up to levels not earned, achieved or deserved via legislation that will inure to their benefit.

This utopian idea is devoid of the reality of life and is the product of the glee one associates with insanity.

THE RATIONALE

The fact and reality that there exists a lower echelon of human beings who are problematic to themselves and others as regards their survival can and does qualify as a primary "justification" for passing legislation that acts to bring down the upper strata of individuals.

ACTUAL INTENTION

The unstated actual goal is to slowly bring down the top and bring up the bottom until we achieve "social equality" where everyone will meet in the middle and we shall therefore all *be equal and the same.* I am sure by now that you can easily recognize "identity thought."

THE PROBLEM

One small point! *It has not ever and will not ever work!* It is destructive of the initiative, vitality and dynamic of the society.

The society runs on the production of the top echelon of able, capable men. Take them down, burden them unfairly and your society will lose its achievers and its heart. The worker is at the top not at the bottom and I don't care what Karl Marx had to say.

Personally I think he missed his calling as a clown because his ideas are a joke. Yes, I am quite capable of sinking very deeply into contumely.

'THE GLORIOUS POLITICIAN' THE PROSPERITY ASSASSIN

Once again the pestiferous "Glorious Politician" has shown his true colors, he is an unlabeled enemy to a free and truly equitable society by reason of stifling the competence, initiative and drive of the top rung of able beings to the detriment of all. Perhaps he is covertly "evilly intended" or maybe just another thrall. This, one must consider, mustn't one?

THE SUCCESSFUL INDIVIDUAL OR COUNTRY

If you are successful, you will be attacked, overtly or covertly – always!!

—⁂—

ARE THERE ANY SOLUTIONS?

Yes, of course there are, there are several.

A FLAT TAX: THE EASY, SIMPLE SOLUTION

What is a Flat Tax?

This is a tax system that applies the same rate to every taxpayer regardless of their income bracket. A flat tax applies the same tax rate to all taxpayers, with no deductions or exemptions allowed. This is really and truly a "fair" way to go about taxation.

Listen for the "explanations" and "justifications" of the irrational, political mind in stating their opposition.

Only the evilly intended among us would oppose this!

LOWERED GOVERNMENT SPENDING

Another simple and easy solution is a reduction government spending in violation of the "first precept of a democratic government."

But, assuming the attempt; can any politician stand up to the attacks pursuant to the downsizing of the government handouts and unnecessary social programs?

He will be subject to: "He stopped…." 'He's denied you…" "You no longer will get…." "He's ruining the country!!" Ad nauseam - Ad infinitum.

He will most assuredly be violently opposed by his fellow politicians who will "fight for your right to live and have like everybody else."

Point to note: The evilly intended will freely use generalities such as "like everybody else" to hide their true intent.

Those who overtly demonstrate opposition to ending violations of 'The First Precept of a Democratic Government." are showing their true colors as enemies of individual rights and freedom; recognize them for what they really and truly are.

AN ADDITIONAL WAY IS A BALANCED BUDGET

Enact a constitutional amendment which calls for a balanced budget and anytime there is a deficit of more than 3 % of the Gross Domestic Product all sitting members of congress will become ineligible for re-election - evermore. This should do it!!!

Lower taxes resulting in more wherewithal for the individual is a function of "less government" spending resulting in - lower taxes! I repeat: "less government spending."

AND ONE MORE WAY IS AN INCREASE IN PRODUCTION

Where does wealth come from? It must be produced. It is the result of activity and the production of goods and services.

What is a product? A simple, inclusive definition would be; A finished high quality article or good, or a service gotten into the hands of the consumer or group for a viable and worthwhile exchange. A product is something exchangeable, it has exchange value.

—⚭—

Production and Exchange

The economic basis is called production and exchange. What is this thing called production? What is this thing called exchange?

Let's look at production. For an individual, he will bring his labor or skills to an activity and produce something that has VALUE! If it is a business, the business will produce something that has VALUE, whether it is to be a good or a service.

Commensurate with the value of the product for the individual or the business there will be an EXCHANGE. This is "the economic basic" and the rest follows and can be established by how well this basis is understood.

ENLIGHTENED LEADERSHIP

An enlightened leadership would recognize that the that the creation and the proliferation of the means to produce new and more goods and services generated by entrepreneurs would inure to the benefit of all and should work to seek the means to do so and remove any existing legislative barriers.

THE PRIMARY PRODUCT
OF THE U.S. GOVERNMENT

Even the U. S. government has a product. The VALUE of a democratic government is established by its product which is hereby named:

"An increase in the standard of living for the individual!"

If the standard of living is shown *by number and statistic* to have increased then individuals in the society will have benefited from good leadership and the responsible leaders will have demonstrated their competence and will be re-elected and the society will prosper.

Without a statistical, bottom line we are left with rhetoric, empty promises and the "game of politics."

A business must have a measure of its success and that is called "more income than outgo," especially if it is going to continue to survive.

The government must show the same; a better life for its citizens due to more wherewithal, an increase in their living standards, and an opportunity to succeed in a viable and expanding economy.

These things can be sorted out and staticized.

ANALYSIS OF THE PRODUCT

Any and every named product requires a statistic to verify that it is being achieved.

Statistic. Definition: A number or amount compared to an earlier number or amount of the same thing. It is a numerical thing that can be counted and placed on a two dimensional graph showing the relative rise or fall of a quantity compared to an earlier moment in time.

Analysis entails, as well, the compilation and evaluation of the statistics of the sub-products which go to make up the statistic. These must be established and verified.

In the absence of verifiable, accurate and correct statistical data no analysis is possible. We are then left with opinion, rhetoric and political pontification.

Anything can be staticized including the aforementioned product of the U. S. Government stated as; *an increase in the standard of living for its citizens.*

Are we better off than four years ago? Look at the graph numbers, are they up? Then yes. Are they down? Then no, by statistic the policies in effect have not worked!

It is my belief that only an enlightened, politician will abide by these evaluations because it forces them to actually find effective policies, plans and programs for enhancing production in the private sector and it punctures the political hot air balloons as it is now in black and white.

—ɯ—

SOME USEFUL,

VERIFIABLE STATISTICS

GROSS DOMESTIC PRODUCT (GDP)

The United States gross domestic product is the market value of all officially recognized final goods and services produced within our country during a given period of time.

GDP per capita can be considered as an *indicator of a country's standard of living*. GDP per capita however, is *not* a measure of personal income.

GROSS NATIONAL PRODUCT (GNP)

Our gross national product is the market value of all the products and services produced in one year by labor and property supplied by the residents of our country.

Essentially the GNP is the total value of all final goods and services produced within the US in a particular year, plus income earned by US citizens (including income of those located abroad), minus the income of non US citizens.

GNP is *one* measure of the economic condition of a country; under the assumption that *a higher GNP leads to a higher quality of living*.

STATISTICAL MANIPULATION

Predictably and indubitably, what you will find come to pass are two things:

One, statistical rationalization: An 'explanation' or attempt to explain away and justify why the statistic did not go up or rise. "We need more time." "We didn't have the necessary financing," and endless amounts of obfuscation and political "BS."

Recognize it for what it is; all are *attempts to explain away failure*! In any successful business the failed, non-producer is relieved of his responsibilities (Not re-elected!).

Secondly, numbers do not lie however; dishonest politicians will *falsify statistics* in order to get re-elected.

Question: "How much is 2 and 2? Answer: "What do you want it to be?" When found they need to be removed from office or prosecuted.

HOW TO INCREASE GOVERNMENT REVENUE

Increases in individual and business production make possible an increase in available government revenue. This is the true way to gain more money not by increasing taxes-much too simple but entirely more difficult!

Government needs to work *with and for* individuals who are trying to improve their lot and find ways to aid them in their efforts to survive and prosper; *and let them get on with it!*

FOR WHOM DO WE VOTE?

Based on the above it is easy to see how today's politicians have veered off course in their efforts to direct our country. They have made "social programs" the focal point of politics when, if they had an "inkling" of leadership and understood responsibility they would know that an increased standard of living and prosperity is a matter of PRODUCTION!

The understanding of "work" and "jobs" is why no politician should *ever* be elected who has no "real world" experience. These experiences can and do provide substance to the credibility of the understanding necessary to be a public servant.

WHICH INDIVIDUALS NEED HELP

Who in our country should be supported, which individuals need help?

They are the producers, the workers, the able, and the entrepreneurs, these are "the who." They are the ones who are having a tough time of it. They are producing the products and services which make for a higher standard of living for the nation. Instead they are burdened with higher taxes and restrictive legislation all in a misguided effort to support the non-producers.

This is not justice, these are oppressive penalties imposed by wrong-headed politicians.

Any politician who vows and affirms that he/she has and presents plans and programs outlined to drive and increase the standard of living for all should be voted for and given the opportunity to demonstrate his/her competence.

Opposition to such demonstrates, at best, a lack of understanding of the role of government and the nature of the individual and shows potentially that he has 'other intentions.'

PLEASE BE AWARE, IT IS BEING DONE ON PURPOSE

If you think that current government legislation is just a result of anything else than a direct, knowing and covert attempt to bring down the able and impose government control then you can count yourself among the "reasonable."

Using mellifluous sounding camouflage in getting programs and legislation passed, these "well meaning" and "caring politicians" wend their way to bringing about the decline of our nation. They are *not* misguided or misinformed; they are knowingly intent on their plans for our society.

Once more, you are warned, please observe, it is really very subtle but little by little our country and the individuals in it are being sabotaged by the supercilious 'Glorious Politician'.

PERSONAL CIRCUMSTANCE AND OPINION

The economic necessities of life compel and enjoin one in productive and commercial activity.

Nevertheless, I am not anyone who would be considered "the rich." I am no apologist for anyone who has achieved financial freedom. By natural bent my entire life has lead me in another less materialistic direction. By my credo, the only true, valuable and lasting richness there is - is *understanding*. This being my most valuable possession and for me, the only one with any true, eternal value!

Anyone who has been fortunate enough to achieve financial success should be validated, admired, and held up as an example of what an individual can do in a free society.

"*It is in the character of very few men to honor without envy a friend who has prospered.*" Anonymous

POINT THE ARROW TO SUCCESS ALWAYS!!!

—∭—

Government Intention: Iteration

Again, it must be pointedly stated that the underlying, unspoken purpose and intention of all government, couched as it may be in the most honeyed, smooth and euphemistically sounding political language is, and always will lead to "total population control."

This will always be at the expense of individual rights and freedom. You are warned.

This is being accomplished "little by little," "slowly and surely," each step amounting to an unnoticeable, slight loss in the freedom of choice and in the decision making responsibility of the individual citizens.

How will you lose your freedom and rights?

It is being done imperceptibility. It is being accomplished at a glacial pace, legislatively, piece by unnoticeable piece at a time and in all areas of your life.

Who is doing this? Why the politician of course!

Smarten up please!

Governmental Analysis

or the Collecting Up

of the Irresponsibility of the

Individual

In analyzing the government activities from the standpoint of The Founding Fathers, who when they addressed religion, correctly identified the separation or division of church and state; the "difference" noted as being a function distinct from governing.

A STRATEGIC PLAN FOR GOVERNMENTAL ACTIVITIES

The ability to "cleave" or differentiate for understanding in the approach to government activities and direction begins with asking the first question in differentiating the directions of approach with regard for the citizen.

To do: *for the individual.*

In doing so; assuming authority and responsibility for the life of the individual citizen, thereby leaving him in an ineffectual and lessened condition and making him a ward of the state, lowering his self-esteem, and making him a true victim of life.

Or to:

Grant: *to the individual* the right and freedom to do *for himself?*

Thereby, and in so doing, *empowering* the individual into becoming responsible and accountable through decision and his power of choice and thence becoming a capable and strong individual and citizen.

THIS *IS* LIFE

The mobilization of life's energy belongs under the control and direction of the individual in the overcoming and conquering the obstacles attendant to his existence. Auto-kinesis is just that!

The understanding of government begins at the intellectual dividing line of: when the government becomes the collective irresponsibility of the individual and seeks to "do" or provide "for" (read; control) the individual. It is at this point each attempt at "help" becomes a lessening of the individual's responsibility to himself and therefore society.

The overall result will be a weak and decaying society, as the individuals will have become dependent, will have given away their power of choice and be no longer self-determined.

Motivation cannot be legislated, but legislation can stifle motivation!

The analysis of government begins at differentiating it from agreements for defense, public works and the planning and coordinating for the *expansion* of survival guidelines; and abrogating the right of choice of the individual by doing or providing for the citizenry.

Please be reminded of the "end goal for all governments."

—〰—

A Fluid Society, Without Limitation, is a Classless Society

Class. Definition: A group of people within a society who share the same social and economic status.

As one can readily conclude there is no "fixed designation."

Our nation is the beneficiary of the many great intellectual advances of Western Civilization, from the Greeks to the Romans and onward to our Anglo Saxon heritage. The United States of America stands as the greatest example of individual freedoms in the history of this world.

Our country, the USA, was established as a Republic by arguably the greatest document since Magna Carta, the supreme law of our country, the Constitution of the United States of America.

We have never had a monarchy or a class of "nobles," nor do we have an "aristocracy." We are a country of immigrants with no titles or fixed, established "class divisions;" steerage never granted a title.

The idea of lower - middle and upper class is an inherited old world idea and is 'Hobby Horsed' by politicians as a pointed indication of the economic situations of individuals. It is a perversion of reality.

The idea of "class war" is the product of the Marx and Engels irrationally flawed and invalid, social and economic philosophy. When anything akin to it is put forth by any politician as a reason for social change or economic redistribution recognize them for what they are essentially, at best - socialistic and at their worst - against a free, democratic, private enterprise society.

The progressive income tax is a product of Marxist philosophy; recognize it for what it is.

Politicians have lost sight of one of their main purposes which is to provide a safe, no-limitation society wherein the individuals can strive to survive well and improve their lot in life.

What dedicated, life-long politicians cannot abide is a truly free society so they impose legislative controls in a never-ending constriction which will eventually yield a strangulation of our country through "population control" and the concomitant loss of individual rights and the freedom of choice.

Duplicitous, disingenuous "caring politicians" are wending their way to bringing about the decline of our nation. Once more, you are warned, please observe; it is really very subtle but little by little our country and the individuals in it are being sabotaged.

—m—

The Solution or "Collective Thought Agreement"

Politicians crave agreement. This form of the thinking process, "identity thought," being the lowest common denominator of reason serves them well.

Seemingly *fair-minded* and *reasonable* thereby easily becoming *consensual*, it can be quickly recognized as the most usual computing method that is being utilized politically and governmentally.

Therefore it can then be *agreed upon*. It is usually justified as: *compromise*. It is lacking in reason, lacking in logical thought and leads to an inability to think clearly: it is *irrational!*

THE RESULT

It is impossible to hold to a standard of reason, to enforce decent and effective principles or even present the lines of good discipline by compromise. The delineation of the guidelines for survival and expansion are not open to compromise. Trying to keep "everyone happy" by compromising is "collective thought agreement" and a political sell-out!

MINORITIES

POLITICIANS REALLY DON'T KNOW BEST

It pains me to write this as it is an insult to any individual to be subjected to a position of a "lesser" standing in our society by politicians by being told and labeled that you are in, and are of, a "minority."

So, with little patience and less tolerance I will be succinct, pointed and unforgiving.

Excerpted from and fully explained much earlier under the heading "ANALYTICAL REASONING, ITS BASIS" I once again point out the following:

The above description of the intellect holds true, without exception, for all the life forms of the human race irrespective of race or gender.

In a society *without limitation* it is up to each and every individual to make his own way in life. It has been this way since the founding of our country!!! It is called "freedom!"

Let's start with we are all AMERICANS!!! If you were born here - especially if you were born and raised here, then you are here with the same rights, under the same laws and with the same responsibilities as we all have.

If you are an immigrant and came here legally then it is up to you to make your own way as every single immigrant has done since the beginning of our country's history.

Everyone immigrating to our country came in unassimilated and many did not even speak the language and it worked, and it worked very, very well.

DO NOT BE FOOLED BY POLITICAL LABELING

Showing a severe lack in mental acuity, those politicians who go about labeling 'minorities' as such, are essentially making them outsiders; as in different from mainstream Americans. It is saying to them "You know you're different don't you? You're actually really not one of us." You're not like the rest of us, your separate; you're a member of a "minority."

"Don't you feel mainstream now and just like any another American citizen? Well, you're not you know, you're a member of a "minority."

Divisive politicians are keeping you under the idea that because you are a "minority" you are being oppressed and somehow excluded by the "majority." This is a lie.

What would be their intention? To garner votes of course. These duplicitous politicians will have you believe that they sympathize with your politically designated "minority" predicament. Again, they will "sympathize" and tell you "what I'm going to do for you."

Hey, listen up - you've got to do it for yourself like everyone else. This is still a free country. You must find and make your own way.

SUCCUMB OR OVERCOME: IT'S YOUR CHOICE

You have a choice when it comes to any perceived disadvantage as to ethnicity, color, or race. You can succumb to it and blame "society" and become a "victim" or, you can recognize it for what it is (ignorance) and overcome it by the application of individual initiative as many, many others have already successfully done: the choice really, is yours! If you don't believe in yourself, no one else can.

COMMONALITY

Race, gender and ethnicity have nothing to do with it!! *You are equipped intellectually the same as everyone else.*

Do not accept the placement and labeling of a "minority" designation as claimed by disingenuous politicians, you are you regardless of your heritage, be proud of it but know that it doesn't define who you are, only you can do so. You are an American first and foremost and an individual in a free country.

In labeling anyone a "minority," once again the "Glorious Politician" has utilized "identity thought" as his "reasoning." It is a divisive, insulting and irrational designation. What could be the intent? To garner more votes of course!

PROPITIATION

Propitiation. Dictionary definition: To win somebody's favor; to appease or conciliate somebody by doing something that pleases them.

This is an attempt to curry favor in a misguided 'making amends proposition' for some imagined wrong. Politicians use this means as a way to ingratiate themselves; it is actually degrading to anyone with an ounce of pride in themselves and their heritage.

This amounts to a strange manifestation used by the "Glorious Politician" to 'buyoff' so called "minorities" by passing legislation in the attempt to show care, but it is really and only an attempt to buy votes. Once again, "Look at what I have done *for* you."

Not meeting acceptable qualifications and using legislation in lowering standards only goes to point out once again, the short sighted look by inglorious, simple minded politicians.

WHO ARE WE?

There are only *individual* Americans from differing places of origin and all of us with different backgrounds. Yes, it is a correct identification when we say that we are all Americans.

Self-serving politicians who would make you feel separate and lesser and represent to you that you are somehow less an American because you are a "minority" do so only to serve their own selfish purposes.

We are all here to be part of a free society and to engage in "Life, Liberty and the Pursuit of Happiness."

In a society *without limitation* we are all free to be *individual Americans*, to flourish and prosper as befits what and who we are as *individuals*. Is this really so hard for any politicians to understand? Apparently so!

Refer please to the "The First Precept of a Democratic Government" issued elsewhere herein.

ALL STOPS ARE GENERATED FROM WITHIN

Look behind you to see if there is anyone there holding you back and if there isn't, then in a free society, one without limitation, the only thing holding you back is - you!

ONCE MORE

"The above, much earlier, description of the intellect holds true, without exception, for all the life forms of the human race irrespective of race or gender."

Someone needs to point this out to you so you can be on your way without a "label." You are you by your own consideration of yourself and without any labels. Make your way as an individual and a free American.

PERSONAL DECLARATION

When I was born here, no one in my family spoke English. I was told to "Speak English, be American."

So, please don't try to sell me any "You don't understand how it is." tale of woe - because "I ain't buyin' it!"

—⚬—

GOVERNMENT

Government. Definition: The system by which a nation, state, or community conducts its policies, actions and affairs. Organization or body through which control or administration of a country, state or city is exercised.

QUESTION

Is the government alive? Can it reason, or have initiative or possess ingenuity? Does it have life, a heart, or possess a soul? Can it create, can it envision or imagine, or dream? Can it appreciate; does it possess the quality or capacity for aesthetics? Or does all this belong to the realm of the individual?

Disingenuous politicians would have you believe it is the solution however, when gone wrong, it is the problem. Why? Because it can do none of the above, only the individual can.

The individual is the foundation and source of the government, it is not the other way around - the condescendingly pompous politicians have it backwards!

A REASON WHY

Bleat: "Why doesn't the government do something about it?"

Q. Why does the citizen appeal to government for solutions and help when it is neither a causative nor a living thing capable of understanding or reason?

A. Because they have been gulled by political derogation from the facts of life and reason!!!

Government as it is currently practiced by its political overlords (in violation of the principles of our Founding Fathers) does not really and truly "help" the individual it actually interferes in the control of his life and acts as a hindrance to him.

—∽—

The Challenges of Life

HUMAN THOUGHT IS THE SOURCE OF HUMAN ENDEAVER

Life is a challenge!!! Being alive does present problems and it is up to the *individual* to solve them. Why? Because it is his life and they are his problems. It has always been this way since the dawn of time and thus it will always be. *It is what makes life what it is.*

Governmental intervention only muddles the natural laws of life! One must confront ones own existence and deal with the unique factors and the necessities of ones circumstances, ones interests and direction. We are all *different.*

EFFORT AND FAILURE

Life is an *effort*; the body is an *effort* machine. The purpose of thought activity is to solve the problems of existence.

The mind can best be described as a servo-mechanism to the individual enabling him to survive to the best of *his* ability in overcoming the challenges posed by *his* existence. Mistakes are merely miscalculations of *effort*.

Failures in life are the whetstones for intellectual competence, advancement and achievement.

Without failure there will be no intellectual improvement as no re-evaluation is possible.

Failure allows for a re-estimation of the efforts involved. Failure allows for a reformulation of the purposes and a refocus and reset of the intentions involved. The value of a failure is a useful life lesson learned!

The experience of life's difficulties will act to mold the character of the individual and act to aid in the development his abilities in enabling him to survive better.

Life does pose obstacles and barriers and the overcoming of these gives freedom for what is on the other side of a barrier but expansion and freedom.

Governments, erroneously seek to deny the individual his personal freedom by eliminating the barriers to life. Thus goes pride, self-confidence, power of choice, loss of the game and the glory of achievement.

The individual has lost the challenges to his life which have been taken away from him by governmental decree. He is less a man.

COMMENT

It is interesting as an observation, the oddity of the high incidence of neurosis in the families of the wealthy. These persons have very few problems.

The basic problems of food, clothing and shelter are already solved, leaving them with very little to do. We would be of a mind that if it were to be true that an individual's happiness depended only on his financial freedom, then these people would be happy.

But, they are not happy. Why not? What is the cause of their unhappiness? It is contained in the fact that: they have a lack of problems!!

The strength and character of an individual springs from the overcoming of adversity. A life without challenges gives no rewards and is a life not worth living.

—⁂—

"Life, Liberty and the Pursuit of Happiness"

HAPPINESS AND THE INDIVIDUAL: A GOVERNMENT DECREE?

An individual's happiness is as great as he can create it. The individuals in a society will not experience happiness from any other quarter than their own generation. They will get the amount of happiness that they can generate, and that is all.

Life can generate *interest* and an object and the things in life are *interesting*.

Happiness is not itself an emotion but details a condition. The breakdown or anatomy of this condition is a function of the individual's *interest* in life.

It is how much *interest* he can *generate himself*; it is how much he can keep *himself interested* in life that keeps the individual happy.

Can he generate enough *interest* to overcome the obstacles which appear in his path on his way toward survival? Why? Because happiness is the application of *self* to existence and that is all there is to happiness!!!

Government can act only to interfere with this process in a misguided attempt "to help." Actually it will not result in help but will amount to, once again, a betrayal of the individual.

Once again it is offered that one must have an understanding of *life* in order to govern well.

REMINDER

In reiteration; the end result, the forward thrust for all government help as regards the *individual* is: "total population control!" Do not be so naïve as to think it is ever to be otherwise.

You are who you are and what you are, and you will always be you no matter the ideas of anyone else - especially the view of the "Glorious Politician" notwithstanding.

Self-determinism may not be cast aside. You must be who you are and do what you're doing in leading your life. It was and always will be this way; except and only when the government interferes.

—⁂—

EQUALITY

None of us are "equal" this is *identification* and denies the uniqueness each of us possesses as an individual.

Intellectually we all have our own identity and differ in our abilities; some are more able than others. Society rides on the shoulders of the more able; advances come from those gifted with vision and foresight; positive leadership in all areas comes from those of us who are intelligent and more dynamic, and we are not all *equal!*

We may, and do however, in any democracy, enjoy *equal rights under the law*, but that we are all equal is once again, just another lie perpetuated by unenlightened, disingenuous politicians who would attempt to deny to you your essential rights.

Excepting the fact of organic abnormality we are all gifted mentally of the exact same identical thought make-up and processes, how we differ is in individuality, intelligence and potential. We are not all the same and we are definitely not "all one," please abandon that idea.

SEQUENTIAL COMMENT

It is at this juncture where I must point out the following; which is demonstrable but unavailable to be perceived by most. To wit:

The much earlier beginning statements with regard to the intellect, the thought processes and the evaluation of the differing potential for each individual, will not easily nor graciously find acceptance with those individuals who have been educated to believe that life is to be experienced as a series of physico-chemical, mechanistic actions.

There are those among us who perceive themselves to be nothing more than a carbon-based life form in a continuing line of genetic protoplasm: and so, since understanding is conceptual, anyone therefore who considers that he is living his life as a biological process will have insufficient intellectual acumen to easily cross the gap into the realm of abstract thinking wherein reason, creation, imagination and aesthetics exist.

The immediate above goes to point out a "super-identification" of the intellect with the body and an inability and failure of the awareness identity of the intellect to differentiate between the two. That is to say, they identify and think of themselves and everyone else as a - meat body.

Aberrant, illogical thinking and mental-emotional difficulty are neither the result of a chemical imbalance nor a synaptic dysfunction of the frontal lobe! What is wrong with the person is his subjective universe. That has gotten into trouble. It is just and only an inability and failure of the intellect to differentiate, note similarities and where correct, to identify things which are identical.

As function does monitor structure however, any severe disruption or drastic failure of the thought processes on the intellectual plane can and will have very marked physical and emotional repercussions and manifestations.

All of this stands as a conspicuous indictment in pointing out the inability of current materialistic mental practices to accurately observe, trace and isolate an effect back to a correct cause.

THE AGING ISSUE

The cognitive impairment due to the physiological deterioration found in the aging population constitutes a distinction based on organic, preventable factors. Aging dementia due to the accretion of beta-amyloid deposits in the brain serves as separate and distinct from faulty, irrational intellectual reasoning.

THE SENIOR FACTOR OF THOUGHT

Prior to an activity is a thought. Thought precedes action, a direction, a goal, a purpose - a survival activity. This does recognize and does not eliminate an impulse, a reaction, things which are done automatically, such as the reaction of removing a hand from a hot stove. However, we are concerned with survival, which is a considered activity and thereby necessitates *thinking and individual freedom of choice!*

—⚏—

THE SELF-MADE MAN

The struggles of life are overcome by the demonstration of self-determinism to the betterment of the individual himself along with the self-same cooperation of others, and in so doing, to the greater good of society. Many strong, self-determined individuals go to make a strong nation. *Self*-improvement is a *self*-generated activity.

Together, united in this effort, we may help each other to survive. Government can exist to provide mutual defense, the rules of order for a civilized society, and the necessary ancillary adjuncts for a flourishing nation.

GOVERNMENTAL IRRESPONSIBILTY

Whichever types of individuals in a society the government recognizes and gives its rewards to, it will obtain more of them.

Validate achievers and you will have more of them.

Reward non-producers and you will create more of them.

ALTHOUGH SIMPLY STATED, IT IS HOWEVER, AN IMPORTANT, IRREFRANGIBLE LAW!

"A state which dwarfs its men, in order that they may be more docile instruments in its hands even for beneficial purposes--will find that with small men no great thing can really be accomplished."
— John Stuart Mill

THOUGHTS FROM THE IDLE MIND (PUN)

GOVERNMENT, BUSINESS AND JOBS

Does the government act in the private sector to hire or to make or create jobs or does it act to inhibit business expansion? Jobs can, and will, only come about in the private sector when there is a need or a demand is created, or a void exists for a product or a service and not as a result of any government initiative.

POLITICAL HALUCINATORY CAUSE

What is the government doing entering into the private sector business arena thinking it can create jobs? A job is a result, a sub-product, is not a thing that can be produced in and of itself. It comes about as a result of a need or demand *for the means of production of a good or service!*

Jobs have come about when innovations, discoveries and advancements enhancing life and livingness occur or when an adventurous risk taker sees an opportunity for fulfilling a need, provides a product or service, is successful, expands and hires people. It is fundamental, simple economics.

Is there a more complex, confusing and totally misunderstood subject than economics, excluding of course government?

THE ACTUAL SOURCE OF THE THINGS CALLED JOBS

Do not be so naive or deluded as to think there is a government agency charged with and potentially capable of job creation, *it is not possible!*

No government in recorded history has ever invented anything, created scientific advances or produced or achieved any lasting, commercially viable production activity enhancing survival. A key point that - survival!

Innovations, new ideas, advancement in all fields are the result of the creative ingenuity of the fecund minds of *individuals.*

Creativity, ingenuity, vision and foresight, these faculties are the province only of the individual.

They are not the product of any group called government: government coruscation is not possible!

—⟋ⷫ⟍—

PRIVATE, FREE ENTERPRISE IS *DIFFERENT* FROM GOVERNING

In today's economy the government needs to step out of the fairytale business of "job creation" and let the private sector get on with it by eliminating the regulations hampering private enterprise.

There is a difference between governing, business and jobs. Politicians erroneously think, and have a misguided impulse, that they have to "do something."

True, valid and inspired leadership will ensure that the guidelines and regulations are not hampering production and if possible, demonstrating a little understood and seldom used restraint of being able to "stay out of it" and trusting the energy, creativity and ingenuity of the productive individuals of the society to get the job done!

A POLITICAL DISCOURSE: LESS IS MORE

"But-but-but you don't understand, my constituents expect me to *do something*! I've got to show them that I'm *doing something*!" ("Or I won't get re-elected!")

"Yes, I do understand. Remove the legislative restrictions and obstacles and get out of their way and let them get on with it and they will!"

"No - no - no, that won't work. We must, must, must *do something*."

"I see your *compulsion*. Trusting individuals to get on with it worked from the beginning of our country. You're the problem now!"

"No! No! No! They will just mess it up and do it all wrong unless the government steps in and takes over. They need legislated government direction and control and only the government can provide that, don't you see?"

"Yes, I do see. You and your ilk have made a mess of things. Let's get rid of every national and governmental program that has anything to do with the care of the citizen like social security (a wonderful euphemism - social *security*, don't make me laugh!). Privatize them all or give individuals a choice to opt out."

"Oh no!!! You're an anarchist!!! We must impose order and control for the safety and security of everyone."

"No, I am a firm believer in the necessity of good government but more importantly I believe in freedom and the good sense of the individual and his right to "choose" and come to "his own decisions.""

If a program is beneficial and well done it will stand on its own merit but this is a decision to be made by an informed individual, let him choose. Otherwise you impose an arbitrary!!!"

"Aghh!!! Because of you all the trolls will suffer. How can you live with yourself?"

—◊◊—

WORK - A CULTURAL ANOMALY

EFFORT

As noted in the very introduction of this work, the body was designed as a biologically engineered, mobile, *effort* machine; it is built for and responds to: *efforts*.

As a result the intellect is always busy considering and estimating efforts; that is what it does! Work can be described as an *ability* to handle effort. When dealing with effort to give one pleasure it is called play.

LIFE, EFFORT AND SURVIVAL

It is apparent and can be clearly seen that the intellect and the body are designed for, aligned to, and are engaged in, the *efforts* for survival.

CULTURAL DISTORTION

There is something very peculiar concerning the cultural pattern of the United States of America. It saves labor, condemns labor and won't have any labor and has to work forward to its retirement!

This cultural departure from survival activity can actually be considered as the center pin of what is destroying our U.S. culture: it is an unwillingness to handle effort or to do work!

—m—

BOOK V

Observations and Analysis

PARADIGM

In order to best achieve understanding for one of the more complex issues of mankind, it would indeed behoove one to seek out and identify the model that establishes the basis for the human race.

Once this conceptual framework has been established, verified and limned; then, utilizing this construct as a base reference the anomalies which account for variations from the standard can now be identified and sorted out for understanding and proper determination.

The inability to conceive an ideal scene for an activity leaves a void only to be filled with illogic, superstition, the vagaries of opinion and most heinously - the arbitraries!

If one has not established a correct and verifiable premise, then no effective correction may take place since there would not be a standard to reference and therefore no stable data from which to align any non-standard deviations. Normally, one would seek to correct to the standard for any non-alignment; true for any case of application in any field or area of life, government and business included. Common sense, really!

—nv—

Joseph Alessandrini

OBSERVATIONS OF THE OBVIOUS

ARCHETYPE

The human race as it exists is made up entirely and only of males and females; men and women. A man and a woman comprise the basic unit of the species: a male body and a female body. These two stylized life forms exist as complementary halves of the basic unit upon which the human race is built and survives.

It is not necessary to understand WHY that came to be in order to understand HOW that is and HOW it works.

As a side statement, since the basic unit of a man and a woman are two halves of the same whole and are a complement one to the other, how can one be evaluated as senior to the other?

Yes, a man is generally physically stronger. But, let us say that if you reduce or lessen the value or importance of the other side of your unit, do you not in fact reduce your own unit as a whole and thereby in the action reduce yourself as well!

What if you pushed affirmation and approbation to your other half? Does this not-ipso facto - enhance the survival of the unit which includes you?

Common sense really, not rocket science.

Take a look at any culture which does not practice the positive as just stated above and you will see that the culture is not stabilized as the basic building block is not strong enough for cultural stability, progress or advancement. It is a breakdown at the most basic level.

This is the natural order of life and any divergences from it are accountable to aberrations contained in the intellect.

—⚏—

MORALS

Morals; according to the dictionary definition are: "Standards of behavior: principles of right and wrong as they govern standards of general or sexual behavior."

For our purposes "morals" cannot be utilized as a standard or be referenced because they are not fixed throughout but shift since they depend on the moral code of the group referenced. As an example; the standards by which a radical Islamist faction views the Israeli State would make anyone in their group who espoused support and friendship for Israel, anathema, and in violation of the moral code of the group.

Morals excite passions, and produce or prevent actions. Reason itself is utterly impotent in this particular. The rules of morality, therefore, are not conclusions of our reason.
— David Hume

What is right or wrong? Depends on the moral code to which one subscribes. For our purposes, morals do not satisfy our needs.

ETHICS

Ethics are contained and are found to be contemplated within the highest faculty of reason and coexist there along with the contemplation of optimum survival.

Ethics in all things are a personal matter.

Ethics are based on what somebody's considerations of their own personal survival actions suggests to be necessary, rather than on what any law says should or should not be done.

The power of choice remains absolute.

BELIEF

Belief is defined in the dictionary as: Acceptance of the truth of something; acceptance by the mind that something is true or real, often underpinned by an emotional or spiritual sense of certainty.

The evident problem stems from one's personal belief, moral code, or religious indoctrination seeming to be "the right way" or "the only way" thereby standing in opposition to the description of ethics.

ABORTION

Since the beginnings of recorded history, rightly or wrongly alcoholic beverages have been consumed by man. Archeological research establishes the consumption of alcoholic beverages beginning well over 5,000 years ago in many different civilizations and cultures.

In 1919 in the United States we passed legislation called "The National Prohibition Act," thus enabling the 18th Amendment which established the "prohibition" of alcohol in the U.S. This would prove to be unpopular and was openly violated. It also allowed for criminal activity to flourish.

Since time immemorial rightly or wrongly, women have terminated their pregnancies. Abortifacients are known to have existed since ancient times.

As with the prohibition of alcohol very strong emotions for and against abortion are attached to both sides. Sound, persuasive arguments can be made for both sides.

Morals notwithstanding, it was, is, and always will be a matter of individual choice.

To violate the practices and the lessons of history will give us criminal activity as the passing of a law banning abortion will not supersede the wish of the individual.

CONSUETUDO PRO LEGE SERVATUR

"The only part of the conduct of anyone, for which he is amenable to society, is that which concerns others. In the part which merely concerns himself, his independence is, of right, absolute. Over himself, over his own body and mind, the individual is sovereign."
—John Stuart Mill

—ɯ—

LIFES DIRECTIONS

One can and does live life simultaneously on many levels and in different directions. Some areas of life are ignored by the individual and some are found more interesting than others and some may find a strong purpose for ones existence in one or another area.

Some examples are living focused on oneself or ones family or perhaps a strong motivation for a group or business. Some of us find interest in mankind (humanitarian organizations) or life forms (save the whales etc.) or the environment; others are more spiritual in nature and find life in the religious realm.

In actuality, the sexual relationship activity amounts to about just one eighth of the possible activities of existence. One can be irrational in any one of these and yet competent and capable in others, it is an individual thing. This one area of a person's life cannot represent the entirety of the value of an individual; it would amount to very narrow and incomplete view.

In so summarily outlining, let us take a look at this *one aspect* of existence which has captured public and political attention and analyze it for some understanding.

THE SAME SEX MARRIAGE

In looking at the design of a female body we can state unequivocally that Mother Nature, pointed as she is in the direction of the perpetuation of the species, designed and made the *purpose* of the female *body*, one of bearing children. This leaves aside the intrusion of the intellect and societal considerations. We are only talking about the *physical purpose* in the context of the continuation of the species.

When a man and a woman unite in the sexual act, the end result will eventually be a new body, a child, a new member of the race. To state the obvious and absurd, two women cannot mate and produce offspring and of course neither can two male bodies accomplish this.

Therefore we can state a FACT: i.e. the basic unit of the human race is made up of a man and a woman.

This was the way Mother Nature designed things in her plan for the survival of mankind. To state otherwise is ludicrous and a fools argument.

Ergo, another purpose can then be verified and established: THE ENTIRE PURPOSE OF THE SEXUAL ACT IS REPRODUCTION. This is a clinical look at the purpose, devoid of all the intellectual and social implications.

A man and a man are the same, a woman and a woman are the same, and a man and a woman are different.

The basic purpose of a man and woman uniting is to reproduce the race.

Two males uniting cannot reproduce the race. Two women uniting cannot reproduce the race.

The above is an observation of the human race without prejudice.

—∿—

LAWS, ETHICS AND REASON

As a supposition, it is considered that the intellect at its highest level of reason would include ethics and consider that ethics would contain the highest faculty of reason in the address to the optimum solutions for survival. We are then left with ethics as reason and the contemplating of the optimums for happiness and survival. (What is the intellect other than a servo-mechanism to the individual in his attempt to lead his life and survive well?)

Although the masters of jurisprudence have made the present legal system into a recondite maze there is still available, to some of us, the essence or basic philosophical principles by which we rule ourselves and it is there, and in the principle of reason, that we can retreat, to contemplate, to find understanding and to advance a solution.

In general, our laws are based on the prevention or inhibition of non survival actions, or actions deemed non-beneficial or harmful to the progress or survival of some aspect of society, or society as a whole.

By deterring, preventing or eliminating those actions that would act to impede the group, society or the individuals in it, the populace can then safely proceed forward in their quest for increased survival.

Therefore, rules and laws are promulgated in order to allow for overall individual, group or societal advancement, as an aid to the actions contributory to improved, enhanced or increased survival.

To the degree that reason and ethics are consulted and applied within the legal framework, the greater will be the sanity of the legal system within that society. Rules, laws and a legal system sourced from reason and ethics provide the sequent effect of a greater survival potential being engendered within the society and thereby being allowed to demonstrate.

—m—

MARRIAGE

The faculty of reason must be accessed in order to sort out the legal aspect of marriage as it is not provided for in the biological realm but has been conceived as an agreement by the intellect and hitherto has been under the purview of both the legal and religious dominions.

For our purpose then, we need to understand that the highest faculty of reason would be the consideration of optimum survival and the providing of the greatest sanity. Based on this fact, we can see that in the context of the survival of the species the union of two of the same gender does not allow for this and therefore is does not compute as rational. If one were to validate this connection legally, it would be the validation of an irrational act as it does not measure up to optimum survival and the greatest sanity.

A legal agreement validated by the courts of law on the same grounds as a male and female union with all legal rights attendant and appurtenant thereto? No, it violates the fact of reason and is irrational.

Two persons of the same gender uniting is DIFFERENT than a male and a female union, it is not the SAME! What is so difficult about that?
\
Remember, that the beginning of understanding starts with the ability to recognize SIMILARITIES and perceive DIFFERENCES.

You have the "right" to be left alone and you are "entitled" to your privacy.

—⋙—

CHILDREN

Male - female physical uniqueness and differences lead intellectually to the development of mental, emotional and observationally specific, gender based viewpoints.

A child, to be reared in an environment where he or she can observe the differences and recognize the similarities in order to establish a role model for themselves as a male or female, must, of necessity, be raised in circumstances best demonstrated by a man and a woman.

The union of two men or two women does not provide the basis for a healthy state of mind, both by skewed viewpoint variance and a missing opposite complementary physical body. In order for a healthy mental balance and outlook to be established during the child's development it must be based on the genetic blueprint encoded for the survival of the species as established by Mother Nature.

This last will elicit the most in fierce protest and rancorous denial in the irrational mind. It must be pointed out however that intellectually, reason and emotion are dichotomies and that sympathy and indignation cannot stand up to a dispassionate analysis of the underlying factors of existence. The protests will be vicious and the counter attacks will produce copious amounts of both venom and froth.

However, the facts are what they are, accepted or not. As a measure of sanity, one must be able to recognize similarities and differences.

Regarding homosexual pairings, two things thought to be different are in fact the same. Two males are not a male and a female and two females are not a male and a female, this is irrational and is a violation of the observable directive for the survival of the human race as established by Mother Nature.

No further examination need be entertained.

—⋘—

MALE AND FEMALE BODIES – SIMLARITIES AND DIFFERENCE: A TECHNICAL DESCRIPTION

As we look at the female and male human body we can see some similarities of form and some differences. We all possess two arms, two legs, a trunk, and a head which are obvious physical similarities. Then, beside the obvious, observable, *physical reproductive differences* we have some other unique physiological aspects of the genders helping us to understand that men and women are different.

The differences start with the distribution of the X and Y chromosomes and leads to the fact of estrogen hormonal dominance for women and testosterone as the dominant hormone for men, these being responsible for our distinguishing physical characteristics which make us men and women.

Then, to go a bit esoteric, even the electrical basis of the genders is completely different. Electrical resistance is measured in ohms and a female body, possessing no life energy, measures 5,000 ohms of resistance and an inanimate male body measures 12,500 ohms of resistance.

MALE BODIES AND FEMALE BODIES ARE DIFFERENT!!!

ABSOLUTES

Mother Nature did not conceive perfection to be the basis for the survival of the human race, only abundance.

Perfection is an idea posed by the intellect and trying to apply this idea to existence poses continual, imponderable and irresolvable problems as it conflicts with reality.

Confusion is the result.

—m—

A Democratic Renaissance

is Possible

SOME GUIDELINES AND SIMPLE SOLUTIONS FOR THE POLITICIANS

THREE STEPS TO AN EFFECTIVE DEMOCRATIC GOVERNMENT

STEP ONE

To be eligible for election one must have lived life in the "real world" of work, jobs, and the stresses associated with the economics of business *AND THE STRUGGLE FOR SURVIVAL AND KNOWING WHAT IT TAKES TO MAKE THINGS WORK AND GETTING THINGS DONE, LEARN ABOUT TRUE HELP AND COOPERATING WITH OTHERS!*

One must know on a personal basis the putting in of a work week, the anxieties of meeting a deadline, making a production quota, producing on an emergency basis to satisfy a customer and the wins and loses associated with a competitive market place.

Start, build and run a successful company. Learn how to manage, develop and hone your executive skills and learn about teamwork. Suffer on up and achieve survival success in a "real world" activity.

No one who has not done so will have the requisite understanding of what it takes to survive in life with its ups and downs, losses, and victories, and most importantly; *the necessary substantive, experiential understanding gained from the practical application of what it takes to survive.*

He must get into the nooks and crannies of existence to gain this understanding. He must work at a job!!! He must produce!!! He must gain and have "real world" experience!!

(Previous "experience" gained as a publicly elected official, in any capacity, does not compute!)

STEP TWO

No one may be elected for office from academia in violation of step one. It is noted that the hallmark of "academia" being, by and large, "intellectual significance" and a general lack of any practical connection with reality.

STEP THREE

And, *most importantly*; no politician should *ever* have more than two terms in any one office; *ever.* This will do away with the "career politician" one of the biggest, if not the biggest cause of all our present governmental problems.

"OH NO, WHAT WILL THE POOR TROLLS DO?

—m—

Conceptual Analysis

"How *broad* is his ability to recognize the similarity of things is." One must be out of the forest in order to see the trees or *to conceive the whole*.

Some of us are "bigger beings" than others and bear the responsibility of understanding that the nation as a whole is made up of "The individual," "The citizen." Too simple, but nevertheless it is true.

A WORKABLE OUTLINE FOR A NEW DIRECTION

The first barrier to overcome and achieve is that politicians must be educated and inculcated with the concepts and understandings of: self-determinism, individual choice and personal responsibility.

Then; legislative activity needs to be undertaken with the intention and purpose to rescind *all* legislative programs that take away individual responsibility and violate the First Precept of a Democracy.

This can be achieved with solutions for a gradual, a 1 to 2 ½ year undoing so as not to cause a sudden stop and disruption and allow for reintegration of individuals to their individual responsibility and to society. No "bridge programs" to be appended.

Total cessation of all violations of the "First Precept" is the goal.

"THE RESTORATION OF INDIVIDUAL RIGHTS AND RESPONSIBILITIES PROGRAM"

This would be an acceptable description.

The target programs isolated, evaluated as to importance and ease of abolition, and times of completion set. Run up time in preparation is not to exceed six months.

Once begun, a zero tolerance for execution and completion needs to exist. Dates to be set, published, and adhered to without exception, period!

Why a zero tolerance? Because of governmental inefficiency and the attendant confusion as well as the predictable outcries and demand for delays plus the orotund outrages guaranteed to stem from the "Dangerous Politician."

The head of this program needs to adopt the characteristics of Draco in pursuit of its execution!

A true democratic government does not have as *any part of its purpose* to be a nationwide amends function and must, must, must get out of the taking care of the individual business. This is the first requisite to a democracy and a prosperous and free society.

ITA EST.

What Will Happen: Prediction

HUMAN EMOTION AND REACTION

When the reversal of the extremely parlous situation involving the numerous existing and ongoing violations of the First Precept of a Democratic Government is undertaken, it will most assuredly create a hurricane of both emotion and reaction.

As mentioned, when these divergences from the democratic standard are found and addressed for resolution there will be without any doubt at all, two very predictable responses both publicly and politically: *emotion and reaction - reaction and emotion!*

PUBLICLY

The first will be the *automatic, individual citizen's reaction* to the change. Any change, even a minor one, will cause an automatic public emotional reaction. This is a very predictable automaticity for just about any area in the life of the individual, and is especially egregious when perceived as being caused by the outside force called "government."

The withdrawal from their addiction to governmental welfare, entitlements and the rest of the governmentally imposed arbitraries in violation of the First Precept of a Democratic Government will cause a public tidal wave of consternation, distress and resentment – beware.

To expect any wide, sweeping social change, even if it is the return of individual responsibility, to go into effect without any demonstrative, public emotional outcry is folly – you dream!

FACT

However, it is to be noted as a remarkable fact the oddity connected to the human experience in that; it is in the nature of a man that he survives *best* when he is faced with a challenging existence!

Thus, he *will* persevere. And in consequence of that he shall resume his rightful status as a self-determined individual in a democratic society.

POLITICALLY

The undoing of the social programs existing in violation of the First Precept of a Democratic Government will be the equivalent of loosening a locked nut from a rusty bolt! Indeed, in a glaringly obvious understatement, it will certainly not be easy to accomplish legislatively nor in the practical doingness of address and application to nullify.

Unable to confront and deal with the attendant emotion to the change being brought about will predictably cause the perfidious political demon known as the "Dangerous Politician" to rant, rave and scream out loudly how bad it all is.

"You can't stop aid to unmarried troll mothers, it is unconscionable cruelty beyond belief. You're Satan!!!" And so forth and so on.....ad nauseam.

It is unfortunate that I can predict and guarantee, without reservation, that all these above will most definitely occur.

THE ANSWER

When you bring order into any area of confusion and into situations where things have gone off the rails and are non-standard it is vital to understand – I repeat, VITAL: that the return to the standard will cause confusion and disorder to turn on, appear and to then blow off. Hear me now: it will cause confusion and upset to turn on in the area being straightened out and this will blow off and it will dissipate if order is continued to be put in and, once established – *the resulting confusion will have blown off!*

WHAT TO DO

Just continue to put in and establish order – never stop – never diverge – never cease or yield to: "We've gone far enough, let's stop here." It's too much too soon, the 'people' are just not ready." "The 'people' don't know what to do, it's too painful, too sudden, too overwhelming. We just need to take a break and slow things down?" "We've gone far enough, it's time to back off."

Remember that the evilly intended being cannot brings things to a completion, it's one of their hallmarks.

Never stop until order is fully restored. Things *will* smooth out and calm down and the society will then be able to proceed in an orderly advance in the formulation of a democratic system. Stability and order once established predicts that prosperity will ensue.

All of this above will go far in yielding a True Democratic Republic.

THE GOAL

We do have a goal and it is this: THE REINSTATEMENT OF INDIVIDUAL RIGHTS AND RESPONSIBILITIES AND THE

CONCOMITANT COMPLETE AND TOTAL RESTORATION OF THE INDIVIDUAL'S FREEDOM OF CHOICE. It is my firm belief that this is a wholly acceptable and eminently desirable goal of and for every freedom loving American individual.

—◊—

Tao Te Ching

Tao /dou/ Chinese, literally '(right) way.'

"When the superior man hears of the Tao,

He does his best to practice it.

When the middling man hears of the Tao,

He sometimes keeps it, and sometimes loses it.

When the inferior man hears of the Tao, he will laugh aloud at it. If he did not laugh, it would not be the Tao."

Lao-Tzu

Current politicians and others will laugh at the "simplistic absurdities," "unfounded opinions," and the "naïve and impractical ideas" recommended herein. If they do not reject and make fun of these then it would not be "The Way."

Condemnant quod non intellegunt

—⚍—

EDUCATION IS VITAL AND ESSENTIAL

We communicate to each other by the use of words, whether written or spoken. If we can agree that our communication can be defined as an interchange of ideas, then it vital that there be a mutual agreement and understanding on the words being used and their meanings or definitions.

Without the mutual understanding of the meanings of the words we use, confusion or misunderstanding will result and the ideas we wish to send will be ineffectually transmitted. That is to say, if the receiver does not share the same understanding of the meaning of the words being used, then the idea or ideas being communicated will _not_ result in being duplicated, nor will any consequent understanding be accomplished. This is especially true of the written word.

An example for elucidation:

"To promote the general welfare."

To: def. Preposition used before the base form of a verb to form the infinitive.

Promote: def. To help or encourage to exist or flourish; to contribute to the progress or growth of; further.

The: def. A definite article used to introduce a noun
General: def. Concerned with or affecting all or the whole.

<u>Welfare</u>: def. The state of doing well especially in respect to good fortune, happiness, well-being, or prosperity

It is not the sound of the words, or the spelling, but the meanings, which result in an IDEA or IDEAS when the meanings of the words being used are understood. What follows, as a consequence, when received by the intellect, will show up as; CONCEPTS!

Words communicate IDEAS! Understanding is CONCEPTUAL!

YOU MUST KNOW THE WORDS, ELSE YOU ARE LOST!

"If you understand the words, then you can read and if you can read there are no limits to your education and understanding." Ester Alessandrini

DUPLICATION, UNDERSTANDING AND THE POLITICIAN

With the issuance of the Constitution of the United States of America one of the stated purposes is as defined above: "To promote the general welfare."

This is a concept which is obviously not comprehended politically by today's elected cockalorums. It is being totally ignored but nevertheless, desperately needs to be duplicated and conceptually understood by these public servants for our society to prosper.

If one understood the concept or idea it would provide a direction to be taken for the prosperity (a successful, flourishing, or thriving condition, especially in financial respects) of *all!* It has been distorted and deviated to "welfare" distributed to a select minority designated by the 'Glorious Politician." There is no substitute for understanding the concepts and ideas, but first you must understand the meanings of the words!

Every candidate for elected office should be made to define each and every word in every sentence of the Constitution and provide, in his own words, a personally handwritten description of what each sentence means in application to serving in office!!

Let's see what you have duplicated and understood; are you clear on the concept?

This would definitely demonstrate a pre-qualification and in many cases also provide a show of ire to the amusement of all.

A BASIC LOOK

Duplication is the foundation for and precedes understanding. One must duplicate in order to understand. Duplication and comprehension are based on having a correct definition for the words in the context in which they are being used. If there is confusion or a lack of comprehension it is generally not the idea that is confusing but either an incorrect definition or maybe none at all, for the words as they are used. It is *always* a missing, correct definition for a word or words every time and nothing else – ever! Period!

One must use a good dictionary, find the definition in the context that fits and proceed. If the confusion doesn't clear there is another or an earlier mis-defined or not understood word or words. It is always about the words, *always!*

To reiterate: "Words communicate IDEAS! Understanding is CONCEPTUAL!"

—w—

A LEARNING SEQUENCE

There is a sequence of learning that goes something like this: *duplication* prior to and attained can and will result in *understanding*; which assembled understandings (plural), when accumulated over time, can and will bring about *judgment,* which through familiarity and experience will lead to *creativity.* You are now master of your own fate!

A STUDY METHODOLOGY

The lack of even a basic technology of how to study is a huge missing ingredient in today's educational curriculum. This void in our educational resources is a glaring omission and needs to be remedied. When the student is told to "study harder" without having the knowledge of "how to study" he is doomed to failure; this accounting for much of our educational difficulties.

—⚊—

SIMPLIFICATION

Education may be said to be the process by which the individual is presented with the accumulated learning's of a long span of a culture.

Education also may be deemed to be a process of making new data available to the individual and causing him to intellectually attend to and use the information. This in itself will bring about reason in the individual.

The goal of an educator shall be to prepare and simplify the information into presentable forms which can be duplicated and understood by the student: in order that he may inspect and evaluate it and come to his own reckoning concerning its meaning and relevance.

If presented in a logical progression to a known result then the information will have been absorbed, evaluated and retained and the course purpose will have thereby been achieved. He will have accumulated a fund of personal information and data to apply to the task of solving the problems of living.

If the material and information is presented as described then obviously the variable in this equation will be the student.

LOGIC

All things worth knowing must be reduced to the elements of their simplicities for any understanding to take place.

—m—

DIDACTICS

A REAL EDUCATION MUST NOT DEPEND ON "AUTHORITY"

Educate. Definition, as it pertains: To develop the innate capacities of; to develop the faculties and intellectual powers of a person.

Etymology: From Latin *educere* from *e* ("out") + *ducere* ("to lead, draw")

Authoritarian. Definition: Advocating total submission to authority, as opposed to individual freedom.

Authoritarian teaching methods by which the data and information is impressed into the intellect and the student's self-determinism in the utilization of those facts is thus ignored and by-passed will render the data into a reduced, fixed state and be lost to inspection, evaluation and utility.

If his self-determinism is to be so reduced, hence his persistence and ability to handle the responsibilities of his life will be reduced as well.

This will leave him unprepared and unfit for the specific functions in his life.

I'm really not sure what the dictatorial, authoritarian methods of the intellectually constipated would-be Little Caesars on their lecture platforms in today's universities are intended to achieve; but by result, truly educated and bright, shining products is evidently not one of them!!

A real education for the individual must not just be the providing of data and information for memorization and regurgitation but; indoctrination in the student of the processes for finding his own answers! *He must know how to learn in order to become a fully educated person.*

Asking the student "What do *you* think about it?" will do more to see that he becomes educated than rote memorization of unevaluated and thus inert data delivered from on high.

ASSEVERATION

An education which invites analysis and the comparison of taught data with the real world will raise the reasoning power of the individual and provide the basis for his success and happiness in life.

IMPORTANCE

A free, democratic and affluent society can only be accomplished and maintained with an educated populace. This is an imperative both for the individual's success in life and the welfare of the nation.

LAMENTATION

The pure white light of democratic philosophy understood on the conceptual level and competently demonstrated by our nation's founding fathers has been diluted, adulterated and abandoned by refraction through a prism of ideology, opinion and the arbitraries and therefore no longer shines on the national consciousness with the intense illumination it so greatly merits.

The fundamental philosophy of democratic freedom is no longer being taught in our schools and is left only to those discerning few who would hold the idea in its purest state.

This cherished idea of democratic freedom will not find greater purchase in our society until it is brought to our children and they are enlightened through the process of education.

"No free government, nor the blessings of liberty, can be preserved to any people, but by...a frequent recurrence to fundamental principles."

— George Mason 1776

—⁓—

AGREEMENT AND COMPREHENSION

I do not wish to cross swords and engage anyone in an assumed contest of intellectual elitism. In writing this treatise it is hoped that it may be of some benefit to others and can perhaps serve to act as a sound enchiridion to those so inclined.

In thus stating, I wish to point out the following as *imperatives!*

KEY POINTS TO NOTE

The natural process of thinking for an individual can be considered as being isotropic by description and *limitless in depth and scope.*

It may then be said that:

The depth of understanding of an individual (perspicacity) can be established by how fine his ability to discern differences is and how broad (extent of view) his ability to recognize the similarities of things is.

This can also stand as a measure of intelligence.

THE APPARANCY OF DISSENT

As you read this disquisition, your opinions and thoughts may have registered disagreement with one or more of the points espoused herein. In actuality you do not disagree. You may think that you disagree but you are mistaken.

As stated above, the intellect is isotropic by characterization and limitless in its depth and scope, and as such, your disagreements are simply an illusion caused by the limits of your comprehension.

If you were able to fully comprehend both the problems associated with government and the solutions presented herein, then you would agree.

So what may appear to be a difference of opinion is really, just you wrestling with the limitations of your mental capacity. I find no reason to, nor satisfaction in, becoming involved with that.

Ave Atque Vale

ADDENDA

DETRITUS

Like a great glacier moving slowly and inexorably over granite rock, pushing forward and when receding leaving deposits of what had been broken away and scraped up, so to, in the extensive look covering the bedrock of government, life, society, topical issues etc. and given the broad scope of the search, many factors were encountered leaving some interesting remnants which had "broken loose." Once the main look of research had been formulated and receded these were left as non-included "loose ends."

What follows are in no predetermined sequence but are presented here in random fashion. Conceivably of some interest or for rumination, existing perhaps as curiosities, it is warned that some are incipient and others may not be fully conceptualized as ideas.

WHAT YOU MUST FOREVER GUARD AGAINST

Since the initial registering of time in this universe, the *fundamental problem for every dominating and/or ruling body*, unseen, unspoken and lying below the awareness of all and yet pressing in its intent from the subconscious; *is that you exist!* The dramatization of this can be found demonstrating in genocide when the evilly insane come to power.

This is not an idle comment. It has forever been solved and will be attempted once again by "total population control." Thankfully, on a planet populated by the "dead forever's" this point will not register and will be overlooked, for oblivion rules the awareness of the individuals of earth. Forgive me for I have taken an uninvited liberty.

SOURCE

Source: Definition, origin; a generative force; cause

Planet wide and in all cultures we have an unanswered question which can be posed as: "Who or what is the source of things?"

This tacit question exists universally, is not openly acknowledged, and yet the lack of any factual answers poses a problem for all of life as long as it remains unanswered.

For those with a religious bent the answer can be with God, The God or A God or Gods, the Bible or a religious book. Some would consider the sun. Politicians who suffer from an intellectual deficit would have you believe that the answer is government. A child will look to his parents. Some scientists would have you believe it is mud; we all came from mud or maybe a sea of ammonia. Many other answers can exist, none of them satisfactory.

All the belief systems in the world have failed to provide any supportable insight or yield a demonstrable result. Count the number of belief systems advanced world wide and you will find there is no consensus to be found.

Man is lost in a desert of mystery concerning an answer. Actually, man is lost period. He does not know that he is; what he is; or who he is; certainly he exists as an enigma to himself. From such a vantage point, or actually, since lacking any vantage point at all, it makes the lack of any factual answer understandable. Thus it has caused him to look elsewhere, outside of himself, for the answer to the source of things.

Without a definitive answer to this question he will always remain adrift in a sea of unresolved uncertainty. Is there a possible answer?

There is. An inversion has occurred. The starting point in answer to the question is contained in the asking. It always has and forever will begin with you. You are the cause, the source, and the essence of your own existence. You exist, ipso facto, by your own demonstration of your existence. You *are* the life-energy production unit.

If You Were Looking For Hell
and Came Upon Earth, It Would
Effectively Serve

TERRORIST ACTIONS

Terrorism exists outside the construct of democracy, the ideas we have of civilization and any known boundary of sanity. Regardless of their ideology or belief system they are the evilly intended, criminally insane. The democratic rules of civilized law do not apply.

ADDRESS

It is the height of intellectual folly, when an avowed enemy demonstrates an act or acts of aggression, to play by a set of self-imposed rules when your enemy plays by none whatsoever. It is a failure to *differentiate* the rights of the citizen from the loss of *any and all* rights by an avowed enemy.

They have surrendered any rights to our justice by their actions and may be dealt with as an enemy of war. Terrorists, despite their dissembling adherence to an ideology or belief, have lost their humanity and deserve no consideration or respect as to their treatment or punishment. Let it fit the crime. Do not *identify*, we are not all one! By their actions they have lost any and all conceivable claims to "human rights."

FORCE AND INTELLIGENCE

These are the two elements to consider in reply to an enemy of this nature. When confronted with an enemy, reason may not apply, however the application of intelligently directed force will.

When applying force in an attempt at survival in overcoming an enemy it must be applied to an *overwhelming* degree and be guided by intelligent reckoning.

Terrorists intend and function to bring Hell to life. Reason, understanding and compassion may, and must be remitted!

Those spaghetti-spined political leaders who cannot confront or handle force are doomed to failure and will cause suffering as a result. Force *must* be met with a superior application of same. In a dangerous world, these are the facts of survival.

ANCIENT WISDOM

"Thus I knew that men's spirit had weakened and that they had become the same as women and the end of the world had come. Since I had witnessed this with certainty I kept it a secret.

When looking at the men of today with this in mind, those who could be thought to have women's pulse are many indeed and those who seem like real men few. Because of this, if one were to make a little effort he would be able to take the upper hand quite easily.

That there are few men who are able to cut well in beheading is further proof that men's courage has waned. And when one comes to speak of kaishaku it has become an age of men who are prudent and clever at making excuses. Forty or fifty years ago when such things as matanuki were considered manly, a man wouldn't show an unscarred thigh to his fellows so he would pierce it himself.

All of man's work is a bloody business. That fact today is considered foolish; affairs are finished cleverly with words alone and jobs that require effort are avoided."

THE HAGAKURE

TERRORISTS: THE HANDLING

A terrorist exists intellectually in a mental construct predicated on violence, death and destruction and which is to be found devoid of any rectitude. Sympathy, compassion and understanding may not be, and cannot be, consulted or referenced when dealing with such. By their actions they have disavowed their connection to humankind and have lost any right to their existence. No quarter to be allowed; they must be detached from the rolls of the living as one would excise a malignant cancer.

When faced with such a defiant, avowed enemy, one must never, ever "Turn the other cheek!"

"But we are civilized and must adhere to laws."

"You are a fool. Terrorists have no truck with civilization or laws."

A terrorist is a self-deluding sociopath who tries to dress up his atrocities by hiding behind the dissimulation of a 'moral right', indeed 'a duty,' advanced under the pretext of a religious or ideological conviction. He is the viciously, evilly insane. Life is better off without him in existence.

Remember, the evilly intended beings cannot abide powerful individuals or countries and will *covertly* work to bring them down and to destroy them.

REMINDER

Defense of the nation and its citizens is one of the primary purposes of the government.

"It is the common fate of the indolent to see their rights become a prey to the active. The condition upon which God hath given liberty to man is eternal vigilance."
John Philpot Curran

The attempt to apply reason and "justice" when faced with terrorism is not just cowardly, it is rank stupidity.

—∞—

Politicians Consider "The Common Man"

Politicians, in general, conceive a dystopian view of the world outside of their heads thus effectively validating their obliqueness and their irrationally conceived ideologies of how to govern.

Common. Definition: (As it pertains.) Without special privilege, rank or status, "the common man."

Only those politicians who look down pitiably upon their fellow man in a public (and insincere) display of "compassion" would consider the "common man" and I don't care who said it.

There are no "common" men, no man considers himself to be 'common" unless that man has been beat down by life and has lost his dreams.

For anyone to be addressed and to be told that he is "common" is not just disrespectful, it is insulting and demeaning.

We are all aware of our individuality and uniqueness and thus should be so considered.

THE AUTOMATON

There exists amongst us an individual of a certain nature who must *hold* himself or herself *back* from any activity because they sense or feel that they will do harmful or destructive things.

If he fails at withholding himself, he feels he will cause harmful acts to his fellows or other areas and occasionally he does lose control and does so. He therefore does not trust himself or his actions.

This situation for this person will of course result in his or her *inactivity, slowness or incompetence both mentally and physically.*

Thus, to enable himself to live, he must therefore refuse any responsibility for his own actions; and so any action he takes *must be on the responsibility of others!* Indeed, he will only operate then when given orders or told what to do; and so, he *must* have orders to operate.

A robot is a machine that somebody else runs!

Totalitarian states actively promote and hope for such wights as they fear and will act to repress any causative, responsible and fully self-determined beings.

Many of these types gravitate to and are employed by governmental agencies - thus accounting for the repute of bureaucracies. You have seen these types.

Passing Thoughts

Inertia, Definition of: describes a situation in which something does not change.

As change is the primary manifestation of time, when a solution is implemented and the circumstances for which it came into being change over time or no longer exist, it becomes redundant.

Inertia or the US is still preventing WWII. This led to implementing preventions in a knee-jerk reaction by politicians and as a compulsion to "do something." (SAC and then AFGSC for example).

The USA must recognize that WW II ended and we were victorious. The barn door was opened and the horse had left the barn. Incorrect reasoning: "Let's make sure it doesn't happen again." Why is it incorrect? Because, it has already happened! (This is an inability to differentiate time or circumstances.)

Law: That which can be predicted can be prevented.

This will not be accomplished by groups or meetings or a committee. *Can this be a purpose for any intelligence/data gathering function?*

Inertia and the depression: The US is still preventing the depression just as surely as Germany is still preventing inflation.

What is the failing? The inability of political and governmental officials including the military to utilizes a mental faculty called - Prediction.

Inertia and trade unions: The solution (unions) to any employee injustices has become a new problem. The idea that companies exist for the benefit of their employees is erroneous.

Every business is unique, the idea that a union can exist to cover all businesses of an industry is incompatible with reality, as it is "identity" think. A valid "union" can be formulated and attached to any individual business each with its own unique dynamic set of circumstances.

The primary purpose of any and all businesses is to provide a good or service for its consumers, its public. Secondary to this is to care for its employee welfare and also the consideration of the environment and the community in which it exists. A successful business will make the owners happy, the employees content, conserve the environment and will aid and enlist community support.

Inertia and the NAACP: One must recognize when the door has opened and cease the successful efforts and change to meet any new circumstances were there to be any.

We know where you have been, where are you going?

WORK TO THE FUTURE

Neurosis: One of the traits of the neurotic is spending an inordinate amount time in pondering the past.

This can be seen politically; at times when ridiculous legislation is issued as an apology for some injustice that happened so long ago that no one is alive from that time. What does it rectify?

Plan. Definition: **1.** a scheme, program, or method worked out before-hand for the accomplishment of an objective: **2.** a proposed or tentative project or course of action:

Direction and concern must be addressed to the future not the past. Life will *always* be lived in the future.

Inertia and Indian reservations. Someone recognize things, time and society has changed and *has moved forward!*

—⚮—

BASIC FREEDOMS IN A DEMOCRACY

Freedom for the individual in a democracy is composed of the following rights. These are some of the treasured "rights" to which you are entitled.

TO HAVE

To find out the things in life you desire to have or possess and to be allowed to freely work for the attainment of such.

TO DO

To engage yourself in a meaningful survival activity as befits your interests, your desires and your abilities. These will often change over time as one develops experience.

TO BE

You have the right to *be!* To be whom you may be in the full expression of your existence; to find out about yourself, to learn and explore life and to grow and expand to your full potential as an individual. Essentially, to be the man or to be the woman as you are. You must be able to, and allowed to, own your own existence.

To find and wear the "hats" of a mate, a social being, as a business associate, as a member of a group or groups etc. and to grow as a person in all areas of life's experience.

Yes, this is the correct sequence. A product must always be worked backwards. Find out what you want to have in life and you will discover the direction of what you need to do to obtain it and what beingness you need to adopt in order to successfully execute your whishes. Et Voila!

All of the above is really just a look and a simple breakdown of the basics of existence and life.

WHAT IS THE PROBLEM?

Problems enter in at the level of government interference through the introduction of the "ARBITRARIES" by the developmentally challenged politicians, who feel they just must, must impose their ideas on the populace.

"THE TROLLS HAVE RIGHTS TOO!!"

—∽—

What Consitutes a Prosperous Society?

In order to have a prosperous society it must be composed of prosperous *individuals!* One of the major goals of every politician should be the enablement of willing and capable individuals to become prosperous thus aligning with the purpose of government which is to increase the standard of living for the *individual.*

Those politicians who can't and won't understand this are self-serving, anti-social and can't think!

Government violations: to not engage in commerce, to not be involved in private enterprise.

In a free society any type of "Social Security" involvement would be a matter of choice. In a free society it would privatized and would be subscribed to, based on merit not legal enforcement.

—m—

Politicians, Guns and
Mass Murder

Pusillanimous politicians when confronted with mass murder, or actually any murder accomplished with a gun, are subject to abject terror and complete, total confusion; both of which are being fueled by their unbridled hysteria, panic and lack of any concept of what to do.

Being thus engulfed, and in a perfervid frenzy to find a solution, they then become *driven by their political compulsion to look as though they are "doing something,"* and as a result they attempt to act.

And being that they are ill-equipped intellectually, they have failed-miserably.

Murder of any kind can never be justified and is always killing by reason of insanity. So really, all they need to do is banish insanity by passing a law forbidding it. A gun didn't kill anyone, a nut job did; the gun was merely the instrument of destruction.

Unable to discern the correct cause (of anything!) and unable to do anything about it, but in mounting a great and furious public display of consternation and lugubrious distress they set about passing unworkable gun laws.

Joseph Alessandrini

There are many statistics and many cogent arguments extant which validate the foolish unworkability of the prevention they are trying achieve by passing the so called "gun laws."

My point is that in failing to come up with any valid, workable solutions they implement ones that only cause unnecessary and unworkable complexity and duress for those not needing to be encumbered with bureaucratic handcuffs.

POLITICAL INTELLECTUAL INSUFFICIENCY

The crazies who wantonly kill cause politicians to publicly and unseemly react histrionically: and to then pass arduous, strenuous and unnecessary gun laws which are oppressive to those who need no such restraints! The sane citizen who knows right from wrong needs no such controls or regulations.

Once again the intellectual faculty of differentiation and the ability to discern the correct cause of things has been wholly and successfully avoided by feckless politicians who can only be described as suffering from 'intellectual ataxia.'

Side note: Perhaps a look into the "medications" most of these psychotic murderers have been prescribed would begin the discovery into their psychosis and establish and yield a "correctible" cause.

—∿—

The Intellectual Trichotomy: A Generalized and Personal Observation

I postulate, by loose characterization and very informally by description, that there are three easily observable and broadly distinguishable types of minds: the open minded the close minded and the analytically perceptive.

IRRATIONALITY DESCRIPTION

In the first, the "open minded," the intellect has too wide a zone of attention. The mind wanders over large areas and is unable to select pertinent data.

In the second, the "close minded," it cannot wander far enough to find pertinent data.

In neither case above can the intellect resolve the problem with which it is concerned due to an absence of data.

The "analytical mind" bears no resemblance to the above two descriptions. It uses a construct of mental focus built to discern similarities and differences without bias and is able thereby to select out and evaluate importance from unimportance.

UNFORMULATED DESCRIPTIONS

The "close minded," as such, are not open to any new ideas but are only interested in maintaining their already conceived opinions and beliefs. Their intellectual scope is limited to only those things meeting their already conceived notions; a narrow and therefore limited view. Nothing goes in unless it fits and is in agreement with their preconceived notions. Beliefs and opinions are more important than fact. Standards are rigid along certain lines. Here, a rigidly held religious belief system will substitute for observation, analysis and evaluation. It is only their viewpoint and what they hold as belief is seen to be valid.

The "open minded" are the opposite in view in that all things are considered to have merit and are to be given equal consideration as valid. They will not distinguish and wish to not be considered 'opinionated' and therefore will hold no or limited standards. They seek to be liked and admired; their wish is to offend no-one. Since they wish to be considered as "fair minded" therefore all things are valid. It is best not to really have an opinion since anything goes. They seek agreement and unless something is recognized as "really bad, by *everyone else*," then it is ok. Standards, if recognized, are lowered to the broadest possible interpretation as all viewpoints are valid.

The "analytical type mind" does just that; it analyzes. It receives and evaluates the incoming data and establishes its relevance as to its importance or unimportance in the scheme of things. They hold valid opinions based on verifiable facts. Reason and common sense are the rules. Opinions can be held but facts will rule the day. They can observe and hold a standard and can evaluate accordingly. They have the ability to see other viewpoints and to evaluate them for correctness.

Since these are just generalizations you will find they may more or less fit tightly only in certain areas. In so saying, these descriptions can provide a bit of help in pointing out what kind of mind you are dealing with.

THE POLITCAL IMPLICATIONS

The "open minded" person will generally line up in the "politically correct" camp and will act on emotion in the political arena. As a politician he/she will include and "think for everyone." An interesting aspect of this type politically, is that it will gravitate to the lowest common denominator in society and seek to handle or include this "odd man" in. It will lean society in an unbalanced attempt at inclusion or equality for the degraded beings and the dregs of society; inability to differentiate to any great degree, everyone has a valid opinion; we are all equal and the same. As politicians they will think for "all" as they cannot discern "an individual" as such. Decisions are generally made on an emotional basis. There is really no real right or real wrong: unable to discern or hold any standards they will vote for "equal rights" for everything - whee! 50-65% Preferred form of government: socialism.

Those possessed of an "analytical mind" will evaluate on the greatest good for all concerned. Factual information vetted against reason and common sense form the basis for analysis. They do not seek to be liked or admired but are motivated more by positive results and effectiveness; goal oriented. The individual is identified and considered as such. Generally fair minded their opinions are based on facts; some views are deemed correct and others are not, all done by evaluation. 20-30% Preferred form of government: Democracy.

The "close minded" person will maintain a rigid, insular outlook, dogma is generally found to be more important than analysis. They will often be found manning the "bigotry brigade." Extremism and religious intolerance are manifest. The only viewpoint that is correct is theirs. 15-20% Preferred form of government: Totalitarian.

—w—

The Universe of Current Politics

In a political world where news means propaganda, transparency and secrecy are interchangeable, liberation means subjugation, help means betrayal, patriotism means terrorism, change means more of the same, and promises are lies. It is here, in this world that our political leaders, lacking even a semblance of probity, feel right at home.

WHAT IS MISSING?

HONOR, INTEGRITY, PRINCIPLES, HONESTY AND DECENCY

"I hope I shall possess firmness and virtue enough to maintain what I consider the most enviable of all titles, the character of an honest man."

— George Washington